Do Your Own Online Surveys

DIY and Self Serve Market Research

Neil Cary

CGW
PUBLISHING

2014

Do Your Own Online Surveys

DIY and Self Serve Market Research

First Edition: May 2014

ISBN 978-1-908293-30-5

© Neil Cary 2013 - 2014

Published by:

CGW Publishing
B 1502
PO Box 15113
Birmingham
B2 2NJ
United Kingdom

www.cgwpublishing.com

mail@cgwpublishing.com

Contents

Preface

I have had the pleasure of working in the Market Research Industry for more than twenty years. During that time I have been privileged to work for household names and blue chip companies as well as small companies and start ups.

Much of my experience in this field comes from working in smaller market research agencies and consultancies, where every employee must be a self starter. Training budgets tend to be small, and unlike larger consultancies, it is simply not possible to draw on vast internal resources covering every kind of research discipline and technique.

And yet, to be able to provide a full range of expertise to your clients, it's essential to acquire a broad knowledge and nurture relationships with other consultants who can be relied on to assist when necessary.

Any profession requires a constant process of learning and development; but in the small agency environment, out of necessity, it is a process of self discovery and to a larger extent, about teaching yourself.

In 2007 I was a founding member of a new market research agency which was established under a leading PR and Communications plc. A significant proportion of our business was providing polling services to PR agencies. While part of our role was to provide advice and support to PR professionals, in most cases, implementing an opinion poll did not require significant research design. These projects were not complex, and while some support was necessary for some individuals to help construct objective questionnaires, I was struck by the ability of many non researchers to be able to create credible questionnaires. They may not have been perfect, and were certainly limited in scope, but they were fit for purpose.

This experience was not only limited to PR Agencies. There were many other organisations (both small and large) who were working to a limited budget, and who had devoted time to questionnaire design, and merely required our assistance to improve the questionnaire, to script and execute the survey (typically online) and provide the analysis. In all these cases, the client had already made a leap into becoming a DIY researcher. Some were more capable than others and more willing to take on a larger part of the task. Yes, we could always add value and provide the benefit of our expertise, depending on the size of the budget, but in many cases, these clients were fully fledged DIY researchers, even if they didn't know it.

That experience encouraged me to set up a means for potential DIY researchers to take the next step, from designing questionnaires in a word processor, to conducting their own surveys. In 2012 I founded Surveygoo, an online survey tool which was designed to provide a full range of online survey tools to people willing to conduct their own online surveys. There are many excellent online survey tools in the market, and while Surveygoo has many features which are designed to assist non research specialists, it is one of a number of solutions which fits within the growing sector of DIY market research, or what is also known as Self Serve market research. We have already helped many people conduct their own surveys with this tool. And yet, we also continue to provide questionnaire design and survey scripting services to clients who, in some cases, could undertake these tasks themselves, given the time and self belief that conducting your own research is possible. DIY research and self serve is not for everyone, all the time, but it is a possibility for individuals working to tight budgets, or simply, for people who want to be actively involved in delivering research projects. The book is intended to illuminate the possibility of doing your own research, and to encourage more people to consider the self serve route. Market research is a good thing, and the more organisations (and individuals) who are able to conduct research, to test ideas, validate products, understand customers and explore audiences, the better.

About the Author

Neil Cary is a market researcher with more than twenty years experience in the industry, and is a specialist in online market research techniques. He created the online survey company and survey tool, Surveygoo, which combines the principles of intuitive, easy to use software with the need to deliver fun and engaging surveys.

He founded the online research company Asia Opinions, and established a community of online research panels under the Opini brand.

You can connect with Neil in the following ways:

 plus.Google.com/+NeilCary

 www.Surveygoo.com

 uk.linkedin.com/in/caryneil

Section 1
About the Book

Unlock the Secrets of Conducting Your Own Market Research

Have you ever considered conducting your own online surveys, but not taken it any further because you didn't know what to do next? Have you started designing an online survey only to give up because you realised there might be more to it than you first expected? Have you previously conducted your own survey but found the outcome fell short of the objectives?

In recent years there has been a staggering increase in the number of survey tools available to would be Do-It-Yourself market researchers. Online research has become the survey method of choice for many professional market researchers.

Affordable online survey tools have become widely available to anyone with an interest in conducting their own online surveys. At the same time, a number of survey tools now connect directly to online consumer access panels, which allow surveys to be run with representative samples of national populations quickly and affordably.

In theory, at least, the ability to conduct reliable online surveys is now available to almost anyone who is willing to spend a modest amount of effort, time and money. It is no longer the preserve of enterprises and market research consultants. With some effort and application, anyone can conduct reliable, effective online surveys.

Key Features

- ☑ Interactive support for the book, including videos and suggested learning exercises

- ☑ Step by step guides for planning, designing and creating online questionnaires

- ☑ Understand key concepts used by market researchers

- ☑ Comprehensive resource, including example questionnaires

- ☑ Practice scripting online surveys with Surveygoo.com survey tool for free

---

i **Definitions**

Definition boxes are used to define a technical term used within the main text.

🔑 Key Points are important in understanding the principles discussed in the main text, so they are highlighted in a box like this. They're also summarised at the end of each chapter.

In this book, Neil Cary, an online market research specialist and founder of the survey tool, Surveygoo.com, shares his tips for planning, designing, executing and analysing online surveys.

The book covers key concepts for learning how to conduct your own online surveys.

Use this knowledge to think and conduct online surveys like a professional market researcher. The book is intended to provide the impetus for anyone interested in conducting online surveys to go out and try it, and to help improve the outcomes of surveys conducted by any would be DIY researcher.

Key Learning Objectives

▶ Planning and designing questionnaires

▶ Sample sizes and audiences

▶ Survey scripting

▶ Using online consumer panels

▶ Reporting and analysing data

The book will not turn the reader into a professional market researcher, yet it will provide comprehensive insights into every stage of the process of conducting online surveys and analysing the results. With practical tips based on the thinking and practice of online researchers, you will develop a clear understanding of how to create successful online surveys.

Use of Survey tools - Free Access to Surveygoo.com

The book is not written for any specific survey tool user. Rather, where possible, it provides general advice which can be applied to any survey tool. However, the user may wish to try out some questionnaire design techniques outlined in several of the chapters.

If the reader does not have access to a free survey tool, it is recommended that they register a free account (Freemium user) with Surveygoo.com. Other survey tools can be used, but the examples in the book will be easier to follow if scripted in Surveygoo.com.

How to Use this Book

I recognise readers are incredibly busy and may not have the time to read every word of the book. It's not necessary to read every chapter of the book, nor is it essential that you read it in strict order. As well as a step by step guide, the book is also a useful reference guide which can be referred to time and time again.

If you are new to the concept of DIY or self serve research, we recommend reading chapter 1 (DIY Dreams and Nightmares) and chapter 2 (A Brief History of DIY Research). If you are interested in using Online Panels, chapters 3 and 13 outline what they are, and how to use them.

Section 3 provides essential background information for new users of DIY research. Chapter 5 provides an overview of popular online survey tools, and chapter 6 highlights common types of market research survey.

When you are ready to design your survey, Section 4 (Create Your Online Survey) provides a step by step guide, in four concise chapters. You may find it easier to register a Freemium account with Surveygoo.com or another online survey tool before reading the chapter, so that you can follow along with the ideas presented.

Chapter 8 examines popular question types, chapter 9 covers questionnaire design and chapter 10 takes you through the process of scripting your survey, using Surveygoo.

Section 5 covers the launch stage of online surveys - how to distribute your survey.

Section 6 runs through the key concepts of data analysis and reporting using typical online survey tools. Chapter 14 provides an easy guide for reading data tables, and summary reports, while chapter 15 examines data formats, analysis software and Cross Tabulations. Lastly, we look at the importance of data quality.

Section 7 is the Resources part of the book. It consists of a glossary, Questionnaire Templates, and suggestions for further reading.

Thanks for buying the book. I hope you get as much value from reading it as I have had fun writing it!

Who is This Book For?

This book is written for anyone who is interested in learning about DIY surveys, and wants to discover how to run successful online surveys.

Who Should Read This Book?

▶ Students

▶ Entrepreneurs

▶ Business owners

▶ Marketing Managers

▶ PR professionals

▶ Advertising professionals

Much of the contents will not be new to market research consultants who are experienced users of online surveys. But if you are relatively inexperienced or have no experience designing questionnaires, scripting online surveys, using online panels, and analysing survey results, this book provides a wealth of practical tips to give you the confidence to become a DIY researcher.

Section 2
What is DIY Research?

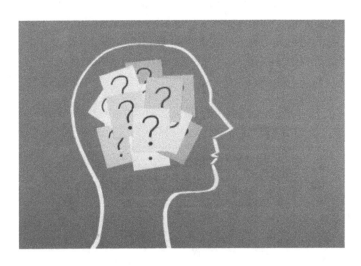

1: DIY Dreams and Nightmares

2: A Brief History of DIY Research

3: Introducing Online Panels

This section introduces the concept of DIY Research.

In chapter 1 we set the scene, defining what DIY research is and outlining the benefits and challenges of using it.

Chapter 2 traces the rapid and short history of DIY research.

Chapter 3 introduces online research panels and explains how their use has propelled DIY Research to a higher level, with fast, affordable and ultimately more valuable tools.

DIY Dreams and Nightmares

> "The reason why so little is done, is generally because so little is attempted"

Samuel Smiles

Dream or Nightmare?

What does the acronym "DIY" mean to you? Most people will instantly recognise the three letters and in all likelihood correctly assume it means "Do It Yourself". The most common association of DIY is of course home improvement. But what else we associate with DIY probably has more to do with our individual experiences of home improvement and our attitudes to the idea. At its most positive, DIY can be a fun and pleasant activity to spend time doing on occasional weekends. It can engender a real sense of achievement and sometimes provides a welcome boost to self confidence. We may also recall positively the fact that it can save money - it is generally considerably less expensive than engaging local tradespeople. And it has the benefit of being an activity for the most part, that the individual is in control of: when to start and finish, when to take breaks, choosing materials, tools and how to complete the project. Yes, it's possible to look for reference material on how to complete a DIY project, or ask for help from family and friends. But for the most part, the individual takes responsibility for planning and completing the project. If the project was successful, you can stand back and admire your efforts.

But DIY home improvement can mean something altogether more negative too. Some people utterly detest sacrificing leisure time to work on home improvement. Their negative views might be firmly rooted in a simple truth - that they are not very good at it, and that the end result is poor and nothing to admire.

In the worst case, botched DIY jobs may end up being rectified at extra expense by a professional, who knows what they are doing.

To a large extent, the ability to work on a DIY project, and to get a good end result is underpinned by the attitude, effort and willingness of the person to learn and apply themselves. It's the same for DIY as practically anything else in life. The more effort we apply, the better the results we get.

DIY market research, as we will discover, is framed by the same potential for positive and negative experiences. Before we introduce the concept of DIY market research, I want to cite another example of DIY, but in the context of online advertising.

Google Ads: The Power of Self Serve

Most people, especially those who take an interest in marketing for their living, admire the brilliance of Google, for developing the search engine model that we take for granted when using the internet to search subjects or to locate websites. Alongside the search engine algorithms is a product that many small and large businesses will be aware of and use: Google Adwords.

Any small business owner has the power to promote their website or products via Google Ads. In many cases, the business owner may engage an SEO or Ad words specialist to set up and monitor their ad words campaigns. In other cases, the business owner, perhaps in a larger business, may take full responsibility for running their ad words campaigns in house.

Of course, the skill and level of experience of the person creating the ads will vary and significantly determine whether the ad campaigns are successful or not. In a way there is something more important than this that we should recognise before considering whether someone is any good at using Adwords.

Google did something amazing with Adwords. They "democratised" the activity of advertising on the internet. Now a small business owner or future entrepreneur could seriously consider launching a new brand, competing with other brands, or start selling a niche product. This is significant of course, because it broadly encourages competition, and allows the small business to compete with much larger businesses.

But it is also incredibly empowering. People have the choice to plan, create and execute their own advertising campaigns without having to rely on a third party expert or internet marketing consultant to undertake the campaigns for them.

In reality, some people continue to rely on third party providers for advising or executing Google ad campaigns, for a variety of reasons. They may not have the time to do it themselves, they may lack the confidence to learn and to experiment, in which case a third party provider may be a better route. But the choice ultimately is there for anyone to use the tools available to them.

 DIY provides a choice of self serve access. The user may decide to create their own projects with the tool, or work with a third party consultant on other occasions.

The same context applies to DIY market research. It is available to anyone who is willing to learn, and to put in the time to use it. DIY research can be done well, or very poorly. Some people are able to apply the tools quickly and effectively; others struggle and ultimately defer to third parties because they lack confidence or a willingness to undertake their own research projects.

Its time to define DIY market research and explore how most organisations and individuals can benefit from it.

Defining DIY Market Research

i DIY Research

While there is not a single definition of DIY research, it is commonly understood to mean online surveys conducted by individuals or organisations, typically via an online survey tool.

The survey software allows users to create online questionnaires and distribute the survey via email, social media or via an online access panel, and to analyse the survey data without necessarily requiring the support of a third party consultant or market research agency.

There is no restriction as to who can use DIY research tools but the most likely users are both market researchers and non research specialists, including consultants, PR, advertising and marketing professionals. Other users might be students, entrepreneurs and academics.

DIY research was perhaps originally synonymous with email surveys whereby the user needed to connect to their own email database, but more recently, DIY research has become more flexible and ultimately more powerful when online survey tools have been used in conjunction with online access panels.

Some survey tools go a step further and integrate online access panels directly with the survey tool, making it even easier for non researchers to share their surveys with nationally representative samples.

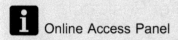

Online Access Panel

Also known as an online research panel, this is effectively a database of respondents who are willing to take online surveys.

The respondents are usually pre-screened against various data criteria, and the panel owner ensures that the respondents are recruited and checked against various quality assurance criteria. Better panels are well managed and given sufficient respondent incentives, attract good response rates.

DIY Research: Friend or Foe?

On one level, the term DIY research is framed by the use of tools and technologies: online survey tools and research panels, which can be accessed as a self serve tool. To that extent, DIY research should be viewed as a channel, a tool, and a means to conduct research projects.

However, DIY research has, for some people (particularly among professional market researchers) a second, altogether more negative meaning. It can be seen as a cheap, ultimately lower quality alternative, to commissioning research via the professionals. In fact, the same meaning sometimes applied to home improvement DIY.

There is some truth to this view - that if a survey is not well planned and executed, it can lead to poor quality research. After all, the survey tools do require a level of expertise and human judgement at the very least, on what questions to ask, and how to ask them as well as how to interpret the results.

To some professional market research agencies and consultants, there is a real fear that too many poor quality research projects will be unleashed, and of course, a reduction in the amount of business for the professionals working in market research agencies. In-house (or client side) professional researchers also see a potential to lose control of research activity, and a genuine risk of market insight disappearing from view, as individuals or departments may be tempted to go it alone and run their own projects.

The truth is, however, more nuanced. And, as this book argues, there are many types of survey which non research specialists are fully capable of undertaking, given the right approach and armed with some fundamental rules of good practice.

At the same time, there will always be a role for professional market researchers, either because they have the skills or experience to conduct a more difficult project, or simply because they have the capacity and resources available. We should not forget that many smaller research agencies and independent research consultants have also benefited hugely from DIY survey tools, enabling them to provide services which were once the domain of significantly larger operations.

DIY market researchers are using a tool. Any tool, if it is to be used effectively, requires a minimum of training and knowledge of how to use it.

Many Users and Uses

There is little doubt that there has been a massive growth both in the use of online surveys in the last 10 years or more, and the widespread use of online survey tools. It's difficult, however, to estimate the market size of the DIY research sector.

Moreover, there isn't a clear distinction between DIY users and market research professionals, since market researchers and non market researchers both use DIY tools. In reality, the more useful distinction is between the experience level of the user, and the type of research activity undertaken.

The experience level of the user varies enormously, from the specialist online researcher in a market research agency, in house market researchers, to a long tail of non research specialists, which could include PR, advertising, marketeers, consultants, business owners, entrepreneurs, students, and academics. Their level of skill and the frequency in which they conduct surveys is incredibly diverse, and yet, all of these groups can benefit from many of the same online survey tools. The advance of online tools in terms of user experience and simplicity has meant that these tools are highly accessible. Of course, some survey tools are aimed at the more professional user (with more features, and more complex functions) but there are a large number of tools which are fit for conducting professional surveys, whether the user is a research professional or not.

 DIY Online survey tools are used by both professional researchers and non researchers.

DIY surveys are used for a broad range of research projects. What limits the use of DIY research, arguably, is the functionality of the tools themselves.

Common types of research undertaken with DIY survey tools include:

▶ Customer satisfaction

▶ Employee Research

▶ 360 employee appraisals

▶ Brand awareness

▶ Product tests

▶ Ad tests

▶ Opinion polls

There are many other uses too - see chapter 6 covering types of market research. But more complex projects which involve specialist analysis is often more difficult to achieve via the DIY route, partly because the types of question are not supported (e.g. Conjoint or Max Diff Scaling Techniques) or because the analysis itself cannot be undertaken within the basic analysis capabilities of the software, or it requires a statistician to perform the analysis (e.g. factor analysis, cluster analysis, key drivers regression). These types of study are considerably more difficult to achieve for a non research specialist.

Advantages of DIY Research

There are a huge number of benefits associated with DIY research. The most obvious is cost savings. If an organisation is able to design and conduct its own online survey it saves on the cost of hiring a consultant or engaging a market research agency.

> If the survey is being shared with a client database, there will be few or no costs for distributing the survey, but even the costs of independently sourced online panels are increasingly affordable, and is likely to be even cheaper if sourced through the survey tool rather than going through a consultant.

Its difficult to put a definitive number on the cost savings because they vary by project size, and depending on the external provider chosen. But if we assume that modest fees from a research consultant might be £3,000 - £5,000 for assistance with designing and running an online survey, the DIY route might cost a fraction of that. In this example, the internally run project might cost less than 5% - 10 % of the cost of an external consultant.

The other key advantage is speed. Online research is a fast medium - fieldwork times may run in days or even hours, rather than weeks for telephone surveys. Moreover, the time to plan and design a survey in house can be faster if only a few individuals are involved internally. Often the process of externally resourced projects can be more protracted, due to the number of people involved in the projects, adding to communications bottlenecks and to some extent, the raised importance of the project, which may extend review periods.

Apart from the speed of collecting data online, most DIY survey tools allow real time analysis and fast extraction of data and reports, with no need to wait around for external parties to generate your data set.

Benefits	Challenges
Fast – data collection within days, not weeks	**Suitability** – online isn't necessarily best
Affordable – a fraction of the cost of a consultant	**Response rates** – can vary enormously
Time – organise a survey quickly	**Quality** – online responses can be of poor quality
Simple – easy to use templates and question libraries	**Training** – some expertise required to use the tools
Reporting – most tools include easy chart and graph tools	**Design** – DIY surveys can suffer from poor design
Support – access to guides, manuals and user forums	**Analysis** – complex data analysis can be difficult with some tools

DIY tools are usually simple to use. Some include questionnaire templates drawn from common types of research project which can be used again, or adapted. This has the benefit of providing assistance in the questionnaire design process, but also speed.

The tools also include a full library of question types to draw on. Some tools provide additional resources to assist the user, such as guides on how to design questionnaires, and of course, manuals on how to use the survey tool. In theory, supporting resources should make the process of discovering how to use a survey tool relatively pain free.

 Online surveys are fast - data collection times are usually measured in days rather than weeks.

Disadvantages of DIY Research

Online surveys have almost become a default tool for many researchers because they are convenient and affordable. But there are many occasions when alternative quantitative methodologies should be considered or are preferable to online. For example, telephone research is likely to be more viable when looking to reach very senior and hard to reach business decision makers.

Trying to run an online survey with C Suite individuals via an online panel is just not viable. Similarly, it is wise to exercise caution when targeting social groups who are not well represented online (e.g. under 18, over 65s or people from poorer socio economic groups).

Research panel owners have much improved the representativeness of their panels in recent years, but there is still technically a difference between the actual population and the internet population.

When running an online survey we need to take careful consideration of response rates.

If you are using an online panel, response rates are less of an issue, because the number of survey completions possible and likely response rates would be handled by the panel company. But if you are sending a survey to customer database, for example, the level of response can vary enormously.

Response rates could range from less than 1% up to 10% or more, depending on the quality, accuracy and strength of relationship with contacts on the database.

 Response Rate

The proportion of people who participate in a survey. e.g. if 4,000 email invitations are sent out and 100 complete the survey the response rate would be 2.5%.

Using an independent database, where there is no guarantee that contacts 'opted in' to the database, risks both a very poor response, and the possibility of being perceived as a "spammer".

Spam

Unsolicited email invitations.

Data quality is a critical issue for any market research project whether it's conducted online or by other means. There are several aspects to data quality, but the core issues relate to the representativeness of the sample, quality of the questions, and accuracy of responses given by survey participants.

> Sample and questionnaire design are quality issues the DIY researcher can directly control, by ensuring that they are done well.

But the accuracy of survey responses is only in part influenced by the quality of the questionnaire. There is also a risk that some survey respondents on online panels answer surveys under a false persona, speed through surveys or give inaccurate answers. I will revisit the subject of Panel Quality in chapter 13 (Using Online Panels).

The complexity of online survey tools varies. But even the simplest tools which have been designed with usability in mind will inevitably take some time to learn.

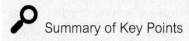 Summary of Key Points

DIY provides a choice: the decision to use online tools on a self serve model, or to outsource to a consultant

All DIY research tools require a minimum of training

DIY online survey tools are used by both professionals and non researchers

Online surveys are fast - completed in days rather than weeks

The representativeness of research panels do not mirror the actual population 100%

A Brief History of DIY Research

"There is nothing permanent except change"

Heraclitus

A Brief History of DIY Research

If you are interested in how DIY research tools have evolved as an idea, please continue reading. This chapter provides some interesting context to the benefits of online research and where it is heading. We cover the beginning of online survey tools, the emergence of online research panels, and the likely future trends of questionnaire design.

DIY research has already revolutionized the way market research is undertaken. The term itself is synonymous with online surveys, as we have seen. It has made research more affordable and accessible than ever before, and it allows non research specialists to conduct high quality surveys without necessarily using a professional market research agency.

Its possible to identify three distinct phases in the development of DIY research:

Phase 1: Beginnings of Online Research

Phase 2: Online Survey Tools - Cheaper and Easier to Use

Phase 3: Connecting DIY survey tools with Online Consumer Panels

Phase 1: Beginnings of Online Research

The beginnings of this modern of revolutions, like so many things is rooted in the growth of the internet. Previous to internet research, it was telephone surveys which was the great disruptor, which had challenged and replaced face to face interviews and postal surveys.

While it took many decades for telephones to be installed in almost every UK household, the internet has done so in barely a decade.

Once organisations collected email addresses, the advantages of internet based surveys were obvious: speed and reduced costs.

 Online surveys are a much cheaper alternative to telephone based research for quantitative surveys.

Phase 2: Online Survey Tools - Cheaper and Easier to Use

Online software became cheaper, although in many cases, still required a high level of expertise to use the software. Since then online survey solutions have become steadily more affordable and easier to use.

The emergence of Web based software, whereby users could access software via the internet rather than buy and install software on their PC, provided a significant boost to the use of online research software. Web based software reduces the costs of distributing software, reference material and updates.

Several well known survey tools then emerged. SurveyMonkey was, if not one of the original web based survey tools, certainly one of the most effective in developing the DIY research sector. Compared to enterprise solutions, it was more accessible, easier to use and very affordable.

 Web Based Software

Web based software hosts the software on the internet. Updates and new releases are undertaken online, which means the user does not need to install any software on their computer.

But while online survey tools allowed the user to create surveys and send survey invitations to email lists, or post a survey link online, they did not provide easy and direct access to mass consumers.

Internet penetration is near universal in developed countries, and steadily growing in most of the world. But in many developing countries it is not yet possible to reach a representative sample of the population, because penetration is too low or concentrated in larger cities.

 Nationally Representative Sample

The sample is representative of the population, including age, gender and region.

Phase 3: Connecting DIY Survey Tools with Online Consumer Panels

The next step in the evolution of easy to use online surveys is arguably the integration of online research panels with online survey tools. A research panel, is as we saw earlier, a group or database of individuals who are recruited and willing to take online surveys.

Not only is it possible to access quality assured online research panels (which are used by professional market research consultants) but with these new, easy to use integrated tools, you don't need to be an expert to use the tools.

Access to consumer panels adds a whole dimension to the power and capability of online research.

Until this point, DIY surveys were confined to occasions where the user had a database of their own (e.g. customer or employees).

While it is always possible to conduct an online survey using a general marketing database, the response rates are often very low. Online panels offer higher response rates and are often highly profiled, meaning it's possible to run nationally representative surveys or target consumers against behaviour or demographics. We cover consumer panels in greater depth in chapter 3.

Although online survey tools have, for some time, allowed the user to create a survey and then share it with an online panel, the process often required some knowledge of creating, amending and using potentially complex survey links. Researchers whose role is to script online surveys for a living would be familiar with how to do this. But to the occasional user, and the non research specialist, the prospect of creating and amending survey links may be too much.

More recently, several tools have provided an easier means to connect with online panels. Some seamlessly connect with panels, so it is not necessary to manipulate web links, or manually set required links (e.g. for screen-outs, redirects etc). At this level of usability it really is possible for the non researcher to access survey capabilities previously only available to the professionals.

Some survey tools connect directly to online panels, giving easy and simple access to consumers.

Is DIY Research a Killer Blow to Market Research Agencies?

Absolutely not. In many ways DIY research has reinforced the need to differentiate research activity by the complexity level and context of the task. Many PR agencies, advertising agencies or internal marketing departments decide to design and conduct their own surveys when they feel they are able to.

In other instances, the range of research expertise and ability of researchers to generate insight from complex data sets means research professionals are always likely to be in demand for more complex projects.

At the same time, tiers of smaller research agencies and individual research consultants are also able to provide professional and affordable surveys to their clients, including for medium size businesses or start ups, who previously may have found research beyond their limited budgets.

In general, DIY research underlies the potential for market research, and creates new choices for all organisations, large and small, to embrace customer insight. To that extent, DIY increases the overall level of market research activity rather than diminishes it.

What is Next for DIY Research?

DIY research will continue to develop to address the needs of its users. Two areas stand out as of greatest interest to research users.

Engaging, Interactive Questionnaires

The first is continued improvement in the deployment of engaging question types, such as drag and drop questions. Researchers know that the most effective online surveys are those which are interesting and engaging for respondents. The days of running long and boring surveys with battery upon battery of matrix questions are coming to an end, or at least they should be. More on question types in chapter 8.

Designing engaging questionnaires is essential, not just because it makes the respondent experience more interesting, but because it helps to increase response rates and data quality.

 Respondent

Someone who responds to a survey. Also known as a survey participant.

It has been possible to design more interactive surveys for several years, but the challenge is making such tools simple and accessible for everyone to use.

Larger research projects, with bigger budgets, already often make use of questionnaire programming which is interactive and engaging (e.g. shopping carts, store shelves, animation, emoticons, etc).

> But too many smaller and, dare I say, DIY research projects, have tended to be more limited and in these situations there is a temptation to use standard and uninspiring questionnaire design (e.g. batteries of attitudinal statements in long matrix questions).

Some survey tools are making real progress in offering more interactive question types so that they are available for all surveys, not just the bigger budget surveys.

 Interactive Questions

Questions which encourage the respondent to engage with the survey e.g. drag question answers, ratings scales and rank order of answers rather than simply clicking on a list of answers.

Another area related to interactive questionnaire design is Gamification. This area is not new to marketers and software developers, and increasingly market researchers are waking up to the idea of "gamifying" surveys. This will inevitably lead to more types of question format, but also new approaches for making the respondent experience more like a game rather than a one way process of giving answers.

i Gamification

The use of game like actions or thinking in non game contexts, inorder to engage users. e.g. by solving problems.

We will look at interactive question styles, questionnaire themes and using the principles of gamifying online surveys in chapter 9: Questionnaire design.

 The idea of gamification is likely to lead to new types of question and approaches to questionnaire design which incorporate game-thinking to the respondent survey experience.

Online Panel Quality

The second area of future development will, I believe, be in the area of online panel quality. Providers of DIY research tools must ensure that the consumers they connect with are engaged survey respondents, who provide high quality responses.

Providing a database of respondents in a research panel is a relatively simple, if costly exercise. Building and managing representative, quality assured consumer panels is a much harder challenge.

The best panel providers use a range of tools and techniques to validate panellists and monitor the quality of their responses. That requirement will only become more critical over time. As users of research we need to know that survey respondents are engaged, representative and honest when they take our surveys. That is in simple terms what panel quality is about. The challenge is ensuring panel quality at an affordable cost.

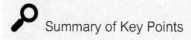 Summary of Key Points

Online surveys are a cheaper alternative to quantitative telephone research

Internet penetration is near universal in developed countries, but rarely in developing countries. This can affect the ability to run nationally representative online surveys

Some survey tools connect directly with online access panels

Engaging questionnaires are essential for encouraging higher response levels, respondent satisfaction and better quality data collection

The idea of gamification is likely to lead to new types of question style and approaches to questionnaire design

An Overview of
Online Research
Panels

"You are cruising along, and then technology changes. You have to adapt."

Marc Andreessen

What is an Online Research Panel?

Lets start by reminding ourselves of what an online research panel is. The simplest definition is that it is an email database. Individuals, known as panellists, have been recruited in to a database, and have agreed to receive online surveys. Some panel owners run prize draws or offer vouchers, while others give monetary rewards for each survey completed, based on the length of time to complete the survey.

Paid Surveys = High Response Rates

The fact that panel members are paid a reward is the reason why response rates tend to be much higher than is typical for a survey drawn from a general database. Individual panels can attract consistent response rates of more than 25%, although some panels achieve a response rate in single digits. That compares with response rates sometimes as low as less than 1% for non panel based surveys where the respondents have little engagement with the sponsor of the survey.

While many of the larger market research agencies operate research panels for their own clients, it is also common for agencies to use survey panellists from research panel companies in addition to those drawn from their own databases.

Types of Research Panel Company

Some panel companies solely focus on providing panel (online sample) services to market research companies and client side researchers. Others also provide end to end research services, offering research design and questionnaire scripting services.

There are broadly three types of Research Panel company:

▶ Companies with global/regional coverage

▶ Specialist panels (e.g. business panel, C-Suite decision makers, High Net Worth consumers, Doctors, Students)

▶ Independent/country panels

Global and Regional Panel Companies

▶ Cint

▶ GMI

▶ Kantar World Panel

▶ Lightspeed Research

▶ Research Now

▶ Toluna

▶ Usamp

The Challenge of Managing an Online Panel

Building and maintaining online panels is an expensive business. The initial cost of promoting the panel to attract new members is expensive. But there are long term maintenance costs to consider, due to the need to replace members who become dormant (no longer respond to survey invitations), or who cancel their membership. This is known as "panel attrition" and may be the biggest challenge in managing a panel.

Poor management can lead to an unsatisfactory experience for panel members. For example, being paid low rewards, delays in receiving payments, being sent boring questionnaires, or surveys which have technical problems.

> One of the most common causes of panel member dissatisfaction is being sent a survey invite, only to find that, having answered several questions, they are then "screened out" of the rest of the survey.

 Screen-out

Screening questions are used to filter out respondents who do not meet the required criteria, in which case they will be screened out (also known as being closed out).

In which territory do you currently live?

- ○ New South Wales
- ○ Victoria
- ○ Queensland
- ○ Western Australia
- ○ South Australia
- ○ Australian Capital Territory
- ○ Tasmania
- ○ Northern Territory
- ○ None of the above

⬇

Do you own and use a mobile phone?

- ○ Yes
- ○ No, but I'm considering getting one
- ○ No, and I won't be getting one

⬇

Thank you for taking the time to respond to our survey. We have already received enough responses for this particular survey, but we'll let you know as soon as another survey becomes available for you.

Example screen-out question flow

There are good reasons why researchers only want to ask questions to a particular demographic, and from an operational point of view, if a survey is being sent to several panels in an attempt to target difficult to reach respondents, it is inevitable that many irrelevant panellists will be contacted before finding the required panellist profile.

It is common for panel companies to invite panellists to take more than one survey opportunity. If the respondent is screened out of the first survey opportunity, they are routed through to another survey invitation and asked if they want to take another survey. It's possible, in this way, to be screened out of 4 or 5 survey opportunities in one session and still not qualify for a survey.

From the standpoint of the panellists who may have been screened out from several survey invitations consecutively, it can be very frustrating.

The danger is that only the so called "professional respondent", who is looking to take as many survey opportunities as possible, will be patient enough to accept being screened out until they successfully find a survey they are relevant for.

Many other panel members, faced with a high number of screen outs, may simply give up. Over time, if repeatedly subjected to this experience, the panellist may simply give up. But it also raises questions of how representative surveys might be if only hardened professional respondents answer the surveys.

i **Professional Respondent**

The term was originally used in the context of regular volunteers of focus groups who were paid for their time. It can also be used to describe panel members who belong to multiple online panels and exhibit behaviour of taking as many survey opportunities as possible to earn rewards.

Motivations of panellists

So why do people sign up to online panels? We have already touched on professional respondents, whose motivation is clearly tied to perceived financial reward.

You won't get rich taking surveys!

But the reality is that survey rewards don't pay enough for most people, and certainly not enough to constitute a decent income. The rewards are intended to provide an incentive to participate, but many panel members undertake surveys because they enjoy taking surveys, and like to provide their opinions. While some surveys can be dull, it can also be interesting to be asked about products, brands, new concepts, adverts and opinions about social trends or matters of public opinion. I can only recall being asked, for example, about my attitudes towards political parties on one occasion, and I found the experience quite invigorating. It surprised me, because by then, I had been involved in designing surveys for some years, and had assumed I was immune to such feelings. Many of us, if asked, are very happy to give our opinions. Yes, answering surveys can be boring, and yes, most of us would become tired of being constantly screened out of surveys.

A number of surveys have been undertaken with panel members to understand the motivations for panel participation. At the risk of generalising, typically slightly more than half of panel members participate because of the prospect of receiving incentives.

But more than one third tend to be panel members for non financial reasons - they enjoy taking surveys or giving their opinions.

Motivations also vary by age group as well - the younger members are more interested in the rewards. Women are also often much more likely to cite non financial rewards as their prime motivation.

It is also noteworthy that it is typical for panellists to be a member of more than one panel. It is not unusual for 40% or more to be members of two or three panels, while perhaps fewer than one tenth are members of just one panel. Those who belong to multiple panels are also relatively more likely to be motivated by the rewards. If we were to use a loose definition, a significant proportion of panel members are professional respondents, in that they are motivated by the prospect of earning rewards.

Advantages and Disadvantages of Online Panels

Advantages	Disadvantages
Relatively low cost	Data quality concerns
Fast – fieldwork coverage in days	Professional respondents
Target difficult to reach respondents	Panel selection bias
Deep profiling of panel members	Recruitment
Multi platform reach, e.g. internet, mobile	Representativeness of samples
Global – multi country surveys	Variable response rates
Guaranteed responses	

 While more than half of panellists take surveys for financial reasons, at least a third take surveys just because they like to participate in them.

Surveys of panellists also consistently show that the optimum survey length is 10 - 15 minutes. Some panel members are happy to take longer surveys if the rewards are higher, but on average, surveys of less than 15 minutes attract higher satisfaction levels.

Types of Research Panel Company

Some panel companies solely focus on providing panel (online sample) services to market research companies and client side researchers. Others also provide end to end research services, offering research design and questionnaire scripting services.

There are broadly three types of Research Panel company:

▶ Companies with global/regional coverage

▶ Specialist panels (e.g. business panel, C-Suite decision makers, high net worth consumers, doctors, students

▶ Independent/country panels

Advantages of Online Panels

Affordable Costs

Online Panels are relatively affordable to use. The costs vary by panel provider, and more importantly, by the type of respondent. Generally, surveys among the general population where everyone is eligible to take the survey, are the lowest cost. By contrast, difficult to reach respondents are more expensive. Examples of difficult to reach respondents would include decision makers in businesses, C-Level respondents in large companies, or mothers of young babys, and much younger age groups (e.g. 16-22).

The pricing of panel sample is usually based on three criteria: (a) the length of the interview; (b) the number of responses required; and (c) the incidence rate, with 100% incidence rate being the least expensive.

 A key determinant of the cost of using online panels is the difficulty of reaching the target (e.g. type of respondent and the incidence level of relevant respondents).

Incidence rate refers to the extent to which potential respondents in a sample are eligible to take a survey. For example, surveys with the general population where we are looking for a representative view of the total population, the incidence rate tends to be 100%. But if we were looking to reach parents who send their children to piano lessons, the incidence within the demographic (parents with children under 14), might be as low as 5%. So if only 5% of parents with children under 14 are eligible to take the survey, the task is more difficult and therefore more expensive.

More difficult to reach audiences (e.g. young mums or senior business decision makers) tend to be more expensive to research because there are fewer relevant panel members, and they are often difficult to recruit to the panel in the first place.

Fast

Surveys conducted via panels tend to be fast. Most general population surveys (or "gen pop" surveys as they are sometimes abbreviated to) are completed within 2 to 3 days, or sooner. More difficult to reach audiences may take 7 to 10 days.

Target difficult-to-reach respondents

General population samples are the mainstay of survey research. But there are many occasions where researchers want to understand the requirements or opinions of audience segments which are more difficult to reach.

For example, a survey to measure advertising awareness of food and drink brands among consumers who have purchased certain products and brands is much easier to achieve where it's possible to quickly screen-out individuals and also to invite respondents who are likely to be relevant. Profiling of panel members (see Deep Profiling, below) is particularly useful for targeting purposes.

Deep Profiling of Panel Members

As we noted earlier, an online panel is effectively a database. As with any database it is possible to hold information about people on the database. In the case of online panels, the type of information held often goes significantly beyond name, gender, age and place of residence.

It can include a long list of data about the panel member's preferred brands, health, use of mobile phones, shopping habits, commuting and holiday activities, etc. This type of deep profiling information is very useful when it comes to targeting potential survey respondents.

The online panel Opini UK, for example, has more than 150 data points which can be used to target panel members for surveys.

- Most panel companies collect detailed profiling information on panel members

- The information is typically collected when a member joins, or is encouraged to complete a detailed profile over time

- Profile information can be used to target respondents most relevant for a survey

The following table lists some example profile data which can be used to target surveys to specific types of respondents.

Personal	Birth date
	Gender
	Postcode
	Occupation
	Education
Household	Occupants
	Marital status
	Type of housing
	Children
	Pets
	Income
	Savings
Occupation	Industry sector
	Employees
	Position
Interests	Hobbies
	Music
	Cinema
	Exercise
	Sports
	Gambling
Travel	Purpose
	Types
	Airlines
	Destinations
	Hotels
	Trains
	Car

Multi Platform reach

Many Online Panel companies provide access to panel members via mobile phones as well as through the more established online route. In some cases it's possible for someone to access a survey which has been designed for the online environment through a mobile device as well. However, online surveys are often too long and feature questions too complex to be appropriate for mobile surveys.

 Many panel companies also hold panels of mobile phone users, allowing surveys to be taken on mobile phones. However, standard online surveys are often not optimised for mobile devices.

In addition to online panel solutions, many panel companies operate separate mobile phone survey platforms which allow the user to configure a survey and send it to individuals much in the same way as an online survey. Mobile surveys have limitations in terms of the number and type of questions which can be accommodated, but if the survey's scope is limited, mobile surveys are a real alternative.

So called 'in the moment research', where the survey is relevant to individuals in a specific context (e.g. a current shopping experience), mobile surveys are a niche but important survey channel. The growth of smart phones and trends towards mobile phone users browsing the internet via mobile devices underlines the need for researchers to be aware of the blurring of online and mobile environments.

Global Reach

The geographical coverage of many panel companies is global, or at least regional. For example, Cint have panels in more than 40 countries amounting to more than 7 million active panellists. It has never been easier to run multi country surveys, often from a single panel company or survey tool.

Guaranteed Responses

A clear advantage of running online surveys through panel samples is that the number of completions is usually guaranteed. If you pay for 1,000 interviews, you will get 1,000 survey completions.

 A key advantage of online panels is that the number of survey responses are usually guaranteed.

This is in marked contrast to using email surveys through a database or a purchased list, where responses are both low and variable. Lets take an example. If a database of 10,000 marketing contacts has been purchased, how do we know that the contacts will respond to the survey invite? The response rate could be as high as 10% or more, or less than 1%. We could end up with 1,000 survey completions or fewer than 100. This uncertainty can be difficult to work around. If we have access to a database at no or little cost, then there probably isn't much risk involved. But in circumstances where the database is expensive to purchase, if the number of responses falls far short of the number required, we would have wasted our money. There is a case, therefore, for using an online panel where we can cap the investment and guarantee the number of responses.

Disadvantages of Online Panels

Data Quality Concerns

Some people remain sceptical or at least cautious about the quality of online research panels. Typical concerns might include, how do we know who the respondent is, and what stops the respondent from making up answers or racing through the survey?

> One owner of a telephone fieldwork unit I know often used to joke that if you want real respondents, do a telephone survey.

There are grounds for being cautious about data quality. Various studies have been undertaken to assess the proportion of panel respondents who behave dishonestly. Panels which do not take any active measures to monitor and control panel quality could see high levels of panellist dishonesty - perhaps as high as 20-30%. On the whole however, most panel members behave responsibly. No one can be sure, because panel members who mainly answer questions honestly can nonetheless resort to rushing through a survey or not answering a questionnaire accurately on occasions. It is for this reason that market researchers take panel quality very seriously, and most panel companies put in place procedures to monitor panel quality (see Panel Quality Management, at the end of the chapter).

Given the potential risk for panellist dishonesty, it is vital that panel companies have in place systematic quality checks.

Professional Respondents

A professional respondent is not likely to be taking surveys as a career, as the name implies. It certainly wouldn't be a highly paid career! But there are groups of individuals who are more motivated to seek out membership of paid survey panels. Typically, they will be members of several research panels and take more surveys. On one level the professional respondent might be seen as useful - they are likely to accept surveys, and we want people to take surveys. If an individual is signed up to many panels, and takes regular surveys, but in all other ways behaves honestly and truthfully when responding to surveys, surely that is not a problem? Well, it can be. Ideally, we want a cross section of individuals to take surveys.

Panel Selection Bias and Recruitment

If survey invitations are sent without acknowledging that some panellists are higher responders (e.g. professional respondents) this can be an issue. Better panel management tools ensure that survey invitations are sent to both lower and higher responders, meaning that a more balanced sample selection is made.

But sample bias can also be a problem if online panels have not been built to represent a cross selection of people. If, for example, they have been recruited aggressively via online marketing techniques which focus on individuals looking for survey opportunities, it is likely that the panel will disproportionately represent the professional respondent. Better panels have been built using a range of online and offline recruitment methods.

Representativeness

it's vital that a panel is broadly representative of the population as a whole. For consumer surveys, in practice this means that the sample the survey is drawn from is rep resentative of age, gender and region. Better panel management ensures not only that the survey invitations reflect the population by age, gender and region, but also that the survey completions are also consistent with the actual population. In some countries, where the internet is less developed, or where poorer individuals do not have access to the internet, it is not always possible to run nationally representative surveys online. In these circumstances, we need to be aware of to what extent it is or is not representative. In some cases, it may be necessary to run the survey via other means.

Variable Response Rates

As a user of online panels we do not normally need to worry about response rates - the panel company usually guarantees the required number of survey completions. However, some audience groups, such as much younger people, much older people or panellists from higher socio-economic groups, may respond less to surveys. Because these types of panellist may be less numerous on the panel, it can take longer to reach these groups, particularly if the survey is disproportionately focussed on them (e.g. a survey of high net worth individuals).

Panel Respondents v River Sampling and Google Consumer Surveys

There are two main methods that panel companies use to reach survey respondents. We have already discussed deep profiling of respondents. Members of panels are usually sent invitations to surveys via email, although some also alert new survey opportunities on a website or smartphone app. Survey invites can be sent to all panel members, or can be targeted against profile information held on panel members.

The second method is what is known in the panel industry as river sampling. Respondents for surveys are recruited via banner and pop up ads, and usually for a specific promotion. There is some evidence to suggest that this recruitment method is useful for intercepting individuals who are not registered with online panels, particularly among the younger demographics. Companies which favour river samples often argue that it is a method of intercepting individuals who are not over-researched, or are not professional respondents.

> The downside to the use of river sample is that it lacks the transparency of profile data collected on the respondent that profiled panels have, and this can limit options for tracking/repeating surveys.

There is also some doubt as to how "fresh" such respondents are, since in reality individuals who are invited to take surveys in this way could also be members of online panels.

🔍 Some online panels specialise in River Sampling, while others use profiled samples. It's important to know which method of survey invitation is being used.

A third, and new source of survey respondents, is provided by Google via its Consumer Surveys service. The Google product sits firmly in the DIY, self serve sector, and clearly aimed at individuals looking to conduct limited research exercises. For example, it's only possible to ask several questions which are very limited in scope. Unlike panel samples, Google surveys are conducted via unknown respondents who are intercepted when browsing websites where the publisher has signed up to the Google service. Google Consumer surveys is limited, but it is cost effective and easy to use.

Panel Quality Management

What determines panel quality? There is no single direct measure of a good quality panel, but there are a number of characteristics which should define how a good quality panel should perform. The panel should be representative of the population, it should be responsive and above all the survey responses from its members should be honest and truthful. Lets turn this on its head.

 Panel Quality

The overall quality of responses provided to online surveys by members of online panels.

What are the obvious signs of a poor quality, poorly managed panel? The most obvious sign would be consistently poor survey responses. Surveys where the respondents race through the answers, do not answer truthfully, do not properly consider the questions and "straight-line" through matrix questions (e.g. opt for the same answer all the way through a grid of questions, simply because it's faster to complete the question). Sadly, poor quality panellists are a reality. One panel company, e-rewards, reported in 2007 that despite stringent standards to recruit good quality panellists and steps to remove poor panellists, around 2 to 6% of new panel members fail their quality tests.

In an article published in Quirks magazine, Kurt Knapton and Rick Garlick refer to three types of panel quality problems:

1. Fraudulent respondents - Panel members who intentionally misrepresent themselves when joining a panel or answering survey screening questions in order to qualify for surveys

2. Inattentive respondents - Panel members who regularly or occasionally do not give full and thoughtful answers, largely because of time constraints

3. Hyperactive respondents - Those who participate in many surveys across many online panels, and who might also be referred to as professional respondents

It's possible that fraudulent and inattentive respondents could account for between 2% and 34% of panel members, and hyperactive panellists could account for another 2% - 25% of panellists.

Panel Quality Measures - Cint Panels

Panellist Rating by Activity

All panellists are scored by their level of survey activity.

Automatic Cleaning

Panellists are automatically removed from panels when their email address is proven invalid.

Random and Stratified Sampling

Within the required targets, a sample is randomly generated as well as being stratified by high, medium and low responders.

Frequency of Survey Invitations

Panel members are given the option to decide how often they want to receive surveys.

Exclusions

When sending sample to studies, panellists can be excluded if required (e.g. removed from a previous wave of a tracking survey).

De-duping

Automatic removal of duplicate panellist members.

Panel Blending

Samples are drawn from multiple panels simultaneously to remove the risk of sample source bias.

Limit on Survey Length

Surveys restricted to a maximum of 27 minutes.

In truth, the size of the challenge of panel quality will vary by panel and by country. But panel quality clearly is a problem, which is why panel companies usually employ various checks and monitoring measures. It's a 'manageable problem' and the reality is the economics of market research depend on finding affordable ways to recruit and incentivise respondents.

Different panels will use different approaches, but most will run test surveys or include test questions within surveys, to identify fraudulent or inattentive respondents. For example, to ask questions at the beginning and end of the survey to check whether the respondent is giving consistent answers. If a respondent is consistently straight-lining through question grids, these so called predictable pattern answers are easily identified.

ℹ Straight-lining

The term refers to survey responses where the respondent has selected a straight line of answers, typically in a grid question, either because the respondent is bored with the question or looking to speed through the questionnaire.

Respondents who complete surveys much faster than the average or is considered reasonable for the survey can also be flagged. Another common technique is to give an instruction. e.g. tell the respondent to give a particular answer or tick a box, to check they are reading the questions. The effect of the hyperactive respondent can be controlled by sending survey invitations to a spread of panellists including those panel members who take fewer survey opportunities.

There is growing evidence to suggest that researchers also have a role in the research process which can lead to better or worse outcomes, in terms of panel quality. The extent to which panel members are attentive and complete surveys thoughtfully is in part dependent on the actual questionnaires they receive. Very poorly designed questions, overly long surveys which are repetitive or uninteresting can have a real impact on data quality.

Internet surveys should offer great opportunities to show fun and interactive questionnaires. But the truth is, too many online surveys are simply electronic versions of paper based questionnaires.

There are some excellent examples of online surveys which make great efforts to use more innovative question styles, and as we noted earlier, the trend towards gamification looks to change the way online surveys are done. But that is the future. In the meantime, many, if not most, examples of questionnaires that I see going through online panels, are long, poorly constructed and often dull. Is it any wonder panel respondents, even when they are being paid for their efforts, can't be bothered to engage with the surveys they see. We will cover questionnaire design to improve respondent engagement in chapters 8 and 9.

One last measure panel companies are able to control is the level of reward paid to panel members. While rewards should be seen as an incentive, as opposed to an income, there is an argument which favours "fair" rewards. If rewards are too poor, the level of response from the panellist will also be poor. The challenge panel companies face is the continued pressure from research buyers to provide lower cost panel services. There is a balance to be struck between panel quality, panel rewards, reasonable prices for research buyers and reasonable profits for panel owners. It's not always easy to get that balance right.

Summary of Key Points

More than half of panel respondents take surveys for financial reasons, although around a third do because they like surveys

A key determinant of the cost of using an online panel is the difficulty of reaching the target, the incidence level

Panel companies often also run panels of mobile phone respondents. Many online surveys are not optimised to be taken on mobile phones or devices

A key advantage of online panels is the number of responses are usually guaranteed

It is vital that panel companies have in place systematic panel quality checks

Some panels specialise in river sampling, while others use profiled panels. It's important to know which method is being used

Suggested Follow Up Exercises

Join an online panel to take surveys. Make a note of the types of questionnaires you find are most engaging and least interesting. Also note the types of questions used. Join Opini panel in the UK (www.opinisurveys.com/uk) or any panel of your choice. Many panels are advertised on Google under search terms like "paid surveys".

Section 3
Get Ready for DIY Research

4: Overcoming your Fears of DIY Research

5: Finding Suitable Online Survey Tools

6: Types of Market Research

This section prepares the ground work for using DIY research.

In chapter 4 we tackle head on the common fears of new DIY researchers. Based on the results of a survey of new and potential users of online surveys, we identify common challenges and how they should be addressed.

Chapter 5 provides an overview of the many types of survey tool available, and sets out simple criteria for deciding on the right tools to use.

Chapter 6 examines common research objectives undertaken using online surveys.

Overcoming your Fears of DIY Research

"The only thing we have to fear is fear itself"

Franklin D. Roosevelt

As part of the research for this book, I conducted both personal interviews and an online survey with potential users of online survey solutions, to better understand how they perceive the benefits of running their own surveys, as well as the things which put them off from trying it, or doing more of it.

The online survey was with 105 UK managers, drawn from all types and size of organisation, covering a mix of customer services, human resources, general managers, PR and marketing professionals. Lets be clear. A survey of this size cannot claim to be anything other than a useful indicator of sentiment. But the results provide some interesting context to the wider issues discussed in the book, and in many ways, confirm many of the personal views I have encountered talking to DIY researchers.

Cost Savings Aren't Everything!

Many people recognise the potential benefits of DIY research, even when they haven't taken the plunge and tried it for themselves. The most obvious benefits readily identifiable are perceived to be cost savings, or that it is regarded as a cheaper alternative. In many ways that is correct.

But apart from the aspect of cost savings (which is often considered among the top benefits) there are several softer, less tangible benefits.

One of the advantages of engaging an external consultant, to conduct any business consultancy including market research, is the ability to bring appropriate skills to the business, but perhaps more importantly, impartiality and objectivity. This is often the case. But it is also true that employees in the client organisation will possess a great deal of knowledge about its products, markets, customers, competitors, that an external consultant could ultimately learn given the time and permission to do so, but on many occasions cannot match in a short timescale.

A great advantage of running your own surveys is the ability to leverage internal knowledge about products, customers or markets, which an external consultant may not have.

Certainly, for small projects, or where budgets are modest, it would be difficult to justify a consultant spending much time understanding the complexities and insight that a more experienced and knowledgeable employee might have about their own organisation. Now of course there are many occasions when the consultant does not need to know everything about an organisation to make a valuable contribution. But it is also possible that small scale projects, which need to be undertaken quickly, could be undertaken more effectively by staff who are already very familiar with the products, markets, and customers. If the project is an online survey, if there are a minimum level of skills in house, to design a survey and analyse the results, it may not be necessary to involve consultants.

Similarly, there is also a case to be made that projects designed and implemented internally can be controlled and implemented more quickly, precisely because there is less time spent briefing external consultants and providers. Of course, that is not to say that all organisations have great internal communications!

Benefits of DIY Surveys

▶ Significant cost savings (no external consultant costs)

▶ Makes budgets go further

▶ Staff know more about their own products/customers/markets

▶ Better control over project design/execution

▶ Good option for less important or less strategic research

▶ Fast - quicker to plan and implement

▶ Generates more internal "buy in"

Not having to liaise with external consultants can speed up the process of getting a survey designed and approved, because there is one less link in the chain.

Perceived Barriers to Using Online Surveys In House

So much for the advantages of DIY research. But what are the concerns and barriers to organisations conducting their own surveys? Motivations for using DIY research, and barriers to it's greater adoption are highly varied. But our survey provides some clues as to which issues can undermine individuals or organisations taking the DIY route.

First, some context to the survey. We surveyed 105 managers in the UK. Half were working in organisations with more than 500 employees, one fifth were in organisations of 100 - 500 employees, and just over a quarter were in organisations of up to 100 employees.

Around 40% claimed that they or their organisation had used a survey tool like SurveyMonkey (either directly, or through a consultant) but more than half were not aware of a survey tool being used in their organisation.

We are not going to report the findings in huge detail, but there are a few really interesting pieces of information that are worth highlighting. First, the wider issue of what is considered to be an impediment or a barrier to using online surveys in house.

Barrier	All sample	Previous users of DIY	Non users of DIY
Knowing how to phrase a question	72%	68%	78%
Making time or resource available	72%	64%	78%
Knowing which online tools to use	70%	55%	76%
Knowing about credible sample sizes	66%	59%	65%
Understanding question logic	63%	59%	65%
DIY surveys perceived as less credible	62%	55%	65%
Understanding data analysis	62%	73%	65%
Understanding question types	61%	54%	69%
Fear that the survey will be biased	61%	86%	69%
Knowing how to plan a questionnaire	59%	55%	64%
Finding suitable databases or samples	59%	59%	65%
Perceived poor quality of result	57%	50%	58%
Budget	49%	41%	47%
Confidence to use an online tool	47%	50%	47%

The table above shows a list of potential barriers for conducting online surveys in house. The % figure represents the proportion who agreed with each statement. Remember, the responses indicate that the respondent perceives a barrier exists, or that others may perceive it exists rather than confirms that it is a tangible barrier actually exists. A higher % score indicates that they agree with the perception, that the attribute can be seen as a barrier relative to other barriers with a lower % score.

If we look at the 'Non users of DIY' column, respondents generally agree that all the attributes are barriers. The other two which are considered to be more of a barrier are "Knowing how to phrase a question" and "Making time or resource available", followed closely by "Knowing which online tools to use". Most of the barriers in the list attract a level of agreement of two thirds.

The least concerning barriers are "Budget" and "Confidence to use an online tool".

But what is really interesting is that the areas which are considered more of a potential barrier in organisations where survey tools have been used internally, are not necessarily considered to be as much of a barrier to those who have no experience of using online survey tools.

For example, we see that users of survey tools are much more concerned with "Understanding data analysis" and "Fear that the survey will be biased". These all suggest that, in reality, these issues can be more of a challenge relative to other challenges. That knowing how to plan a questionnaire, to use appropriate questions, or finding suitable databases, are less of a concern than analysing survey results. Yet, at the same time, users are less concerned that "DIY surveys (are) perceived as less credible (than using external consultants)".

Among previous users of DIY, knowing how to plan a questionnaire, to use appropriate questions or finding suitable databases, are less of a concern than the task of analysing survey results.

It's important to note here that we cannot judge whether these sentiments are correct. We don't know how proficient or knowledgeable the people in the survey are. But it does suggest that even among users of survey tools, there remain significant concerns on the wider barriers to using survey tools. Most barriers attract a level of agreement of more than half of the sample of users. So to that extent, all of the barriers measured in the survey are considered to be a concern, and it is these concerns which I plan to address in this book.

Everyone Can Do Questionnaire Design, Can't They?

In our survey we asked respondents to consider a list of tasks connected to planning and conducting online surveys in house. They were then asked to rank the tasks, with those they felt could be handled most capably by their organisation internally, at the top, and least capably at the bottom.

The number 1 ranking was shared between "Managing a team working on the survey" and "Deciding when to use internal resources or use outside consultants".

The second ranking position was "Planning research objectives" followed closely by "Questionnaire Design". The third ranking was shared between "Planning research design" and again "Questionnaire Design".

The next middle tier of ranking positions (4, 5 and 6) again included "Planning research design" and "Managing a team", as well as "Analysis and Reporting".

The lowest ranks (7,8 and 9) included "Evaluating Survey Software" and "Scripting Online surveys via a Survey Tool".

So there we have it. Organisations feel they are better suited at planning and managing research than conducting it. But at the same time, many organisations feel they are capable of designing a questionnaire, even if they don't feel comfortable turning that questionnaire into a live online survey.

In a way this is a simple summary I can agree with, that many people are capable of designing a questionnaire, with some discipline and effort. But I also think it is possible to go beyond that: scripting online surveys, collating and analysing the results.

In House Survey Capabilities

▶ Top Ranking Capabilities

▶ Managing a team working on a survey

▶ Deciding when to use internal resource or outside consultants

▶ Planning research objectives

▶ Planning research design

▶ Questionnaire design

▶ Middle Ranking Capabilities

▶ Managing a team working on the survey design

▶ Planning research design

▶ Analysis and reporting

▶ Scripting online surveys via a Survey tool

▶ Low Ranking Capabilities

▶ Evaluating Survey software

▶ Scripting online surveys via a Survey tool

Summary of Key Points

A great advantage of running your own surveys is the ability to leverage internal knowledge about products, customers or markets, which an external consultant may not have

Not having it liaise with external consultants can speed up the process of getting a survey designed and approved, because there is one less link in the chain

Among previous users of of DIY, knowing how to plan a questionnaire, to use appropriate questions or finding suitable databases, are often less of a concern than the task of analysing survey results

Finding Suitable
Online Survey Tools

Online surveys are one of the main methods for conducting market research today. There are so many survey tools available that it is difficult to keep track of them all. Some tools are clearly aimed at expert or professional users, while others are more affordable, perhaps with fewer features. Arguably, even the more affordable online tools now typically offer features which only high end tools offered 10 years or even 5 years ago.

As we saw earlier, the distinction between professional research and DIY research has blurred in recent years. There are times when professional researchers use survey tools which a non research professional can also access. Many survey tools also now connect with online research panels, many of which are also used by professional researchers.

There are many examples of free survey tools, or tools which offer a limited, free trial period. If you have never looked at survey software before, simply search for "online survey tools" or "free survey tools" in Google.

There are so many providers, each with different strengths and selling points, it's simply not possible to cover them all here.

Free survey tools usually have limitations in terms of number of responses, availability of questionnaire templates, number or types of questions available. They are often suitable for a small survey (e.g. internal staff survey) but arguably, are more useful as a low risk way to assess the suitability of a survey tool before committing to a subscription.

Examples of Survey Tools

www.surveymonkey.com

www.surveygizmo.com

www.surveygoo.com

www.dotsurvey.com

www.google.com/insights/consumersurveys/home

www.snapsurveys.com

www.surveyshack.com

www.keysurvey.co.uk

www.fluidsurveys.com

www.qualtrics.com

How to Choose Which Survey Solution is Right for You

Many of the survey tools available will have similar features. Higher end survey tools should incorporate the ability to set sample quotas, and are more likely to have a broader range of question types. They will also have more complex question routing and question piping capabilities.

Quotas allow the user to set an upper limit for the number of survey responses. e.g. set parameters to achieve a set number of interviews by age, gender, region, income level, profession. If we don't set quotas, then the number of responses may fall naturally, which could mean getting too few responses for all the desired groups.

Higher end survey tools will also have a much larger range of question types. Increasingly, however, even more affordable tools are offering more question types. The emerging trend of gamification is changing the way researchers design questionnaires. Some of the higher end tools are better equipped to create gamification style questionnaires, although it is likely more affordable survey tools will also introduce these types of question to reflect market demand. Moreover, gamification is not just about using wizzy questions - it is also about how questions are phrased.

We will cover gamification in detail in chapters 8 and 9.

Routing is often a requirement for even the most basic survey. Routing, or skip logic, as it is sometimes called, ensures that a respondent is asked specific questions based on previous answers given in the questionnaire. Most survey tools will offer this function, although more sophisticated tools will offer the ability to include advanced and more complex routing combinations.

Similarly, higher end tools have advanced capabilities for piping. Piping refers to porting through specific answers to another question. For example, if we asked a question, Which brand of mobile phone do you currently use, we could bring the name of the brand through to the next question, which asks, how likely are you to continue using brand "x" (brand x would have been referenced from the previous question).

There are many other distinguishing features of survey tools including data reports, data export options, questionnaire templates, ability to brand surveys and choice of background themes.

 Background Themes

Many survey tools allow the user to change the look and feel of the survey by choosing from a template survey design, to make the survey look more appealing.

Whether you require a more complex survey tool, or a more affordable solution will be driven by the type of survey you need to undertake, and how often you will need to design surveys. If you requirement is less complicated, then it is likely that a more affordable survey tool would be a better fit. Since many survey tools offer free or trial use, it's possible to try out a few alternatives to see which is best for you. Some survey tools also allow limited subscription periods, or pay as you go options, which means it's not necessary to be locked into a long subscription period.

Another feature of some of the more advanced survey tools is that they may be available as software which is installed on a computer. The main advantage being that if the internet is down (yes, we all know that internet access is not 100% reliable) the user can continue to work designing a questionnaire or analysing data. The disadvantage is that updates to the software will need to be done manually, and the survey license will be limited to the computer.

In reality, advanced survey tools are considerably more expensive, and will require significant time and expertise to use. In that sense, they are not ideal for the occasional survey user, or the DIY researcher. As with most things in life, there is a happy trade off to be found between cost and quality. Less advanced tools are often designed for less advanced users (although not exclusively). The better examples have simple user interfaces, avoid complex research terminology, have clear steps for designing questionnaires and are more intuitive.

Steps for Evaluating Survey Tools

▶ Draw up a shortlist

▶ Review reference material

▶ Design a draft questionnaire

▶ Test run a survey

▶ Review data reports and outputs

 More advanced survey tools not only are more expensive, but typically require more time and expertise to master.

1. Draw Up a Shortlist

Although it's possible to register free trials with multiple survey tools, from a practical point of view, there are time considerations for evaluating too many alternatives.

Having decided whether you will need a more sophisticated solution or a simpler tool, and of course, what budget you have, make a short list of providers. Ensure you look for the minimum features you will need, and the commercial terms of the tool (e.g. length of subscription term, cost per month, etc).

A simple list of evaluation criteria might look like this:

- ☑ Number of questions

- ☑ Number of responses

- ☑ Question types (standard and advanced)

- ☑ Survey invitation/sharing methods

- ☑ Access/integrated access to online panels

- ☑ Routing/piping capabilities

- ☑ Tutorials/guides

- ☑ Reference material/support forums

- ☑ Questionnaire/Theme templates

- ☑ Outputs/reports

- ☑ Cost/subscription terms

It's tempting to add to the evaluation criteria, but if it gets too long, it will make the decision making harder. Of course, include the criteria which is most relevant to you or your organisation. For example, the ability to install the software on a local sever or computer might be more important to you (or your IT manager!) than other functionality. In the end, the evaluation criteria needs to be relevant to you, or the ultimate user.

When drawing up a shortlist of potential survey tools, make sure you use evaluation criteria which are relevant to you or your organisation's circumstances.

2. Review Reference Material

Next, take some time to look at the tutorials and resources available on the website of the survey tool. Many will offer videos (virtual tours and walk-throughs), tutorials, guides and support forums. This should give a good overview of the capabilities, and crucially, the difficulty level of learning to use the tool. Some tools offer a range of articles and how to resources to help a new user. Surveygoo for example, provides various articles on research issues, a blog and a support forum, all of which are designed to provide useful reference material and help, and could be particularly valuable to the less experienced, DIY researcher.

3. Design a Draft Questionnaire

You may not have a survey ready to go, or may not be very familiar yet with questionnaire design, but this is a great way to get a feel for a survey tool. Does it seem complicated? Are you able to quickly identify the different question types available? Do they seem easy to set up? For the less experienced DIY researcher, the overall look, and feel of a survey tool is incredibly important. If it doesn't put you off, you have a much greater chance of staying with the task of designing your own surveys.

If you want to take sometime to review question types (in chapter 8) then now is a good time to do so. It will help you evaluate if there are any key question types available, or missing in the survey tool you are considering. But for the purposes of getting a feel for a survey tool, arguably it's better to jump right in.

Of course, if you are a more experienced DIY researcher (e.g. you have some experience of designing questionnaires, or have used other survey tools before) than it would make sense to design the type of questionnaire you are used to. It may be that traditional and familiar question types (e.g. multi-code questions, or matrix questions) are perfectly adequate for the task. But it is also worth reviewing what other types of more advanced questions are possible too.

 The best way to see if a survey tool is right for you is to register and give it a try. The overall feel and look of a tool is arguably as important as it's functionality. If it seems to complicated, and it puts you off trying it, the chances are you will not enjoy using it.

4. Test Run a Survey

If the survey tool includes a free trial or free use option, it is a good idea to take advantage of it. The free use option may have sufficient capabilities to run a live survey (e.g. with employees or customers) but resist the temptation to launch a survey without doing a test run, where only you will complete the survey. The easiest way of doing this is to set up the trial sample (database list) with your own email address. Either set up a survey from scratch, or make use of a questionnaire template, if the survey tool includes this option. You can always use a template to get started, and then modify or add questions. The survey can either be sent as an email invitation, or in most cases, you can preview the survey or access the survey link from within the survey tool. Whether you choose to look at question routing is optional, depending on the complexity of the test questionnaire. It is a good idea to satisfy yourself that routing functionality is sufficient for your needs, and doesn't take a PhD in computer programming to set up!

 Always test run a survey, using you as the target audience. If you are in a hurry, it is quicker to use existing questionnaire templates available in the survey tool.

5. Review Data Reports and Outputs

Having completed your test survey you are ready to look at the reporting outputs of the survey tool. Although the test survey many only have one completion (yours!) that is all you need to get an idea of what report outputs will look like, and how easy it is to understand them. Surveygoo, as an example, provides various levels of data outputs. The simplest outputs are a summary report (pdf document) and data tables, accessible in Excel. It also features a dashboard view which lets the user drill into the survey results from the account login.

As a DIY Researcher, you may have quite a lot of experience of reading data, or virtually none at all. So it's very important that the outputs available from the survey tool are right for you. Even if you do not need to use the more advanced capabilities that a tool may offer, the minimum outputs need to be fit for purpose, and easy to access.

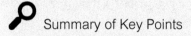 Summary of Key Points

Free survey tools usually have limitations in terms of number of responses, availability of questionnaire templates, number or type of questions available. They are often suitable for a small survey (e.g. internal staff survey) but arguably, are more useful as a low risk way to assess the suitability of a survey tool before committing to a subscription

More advanced survey tools not only are more expensive, but typically require more time and expertise to master

When drawing up a shortlist of potential survey tools, make sure you use evaluation criteria which are relevant to you or your organisation's circumstances

The best way to see if a survey tool is right for you is to register and give it a try. The overall feel and look of a tool is arguably as important as it's functionality. If it seems too complicated, and puts you off using it, the chances are you will not enjoy using it

Always test run a survey, using you as the audience. If you are in a hurry, it is quicker to use existing questionnaire templates available in the survey tool

Suggested Follow Up Exercises

Make a list of criteria to evaluate survey tools

Register with a survey tool and use a free/trial option. We recommend registering a Freemium subscription with www.surveygoo.com

evaluate question types - refer to quick guide overview of question types at:

www.surveygoo.com/page/quickguidetutorial

Set up draft questions

Design and launch a test survey

Common Types of
Online Surveys

Online market research can be used for a multitude of business objectives. I use the term business objectives deliberately here rather than the often used term, research objectives. In the end any research we undertake must relate to specific business (or organisation) objectives.

The information we collect must be part of a considered plan to obtain feedback from customers or the markets we target, which is both relevant and will enable actions. It's what researchers sometimes call 'actionable data'.

 Actionable Data

The objective of collecting data through market research which highlights or clarifies opportunities to take firm business decisions.

Of course, not every single piece of data or feedback we collect from a single survey can result in a direct business action, but taken as a whole, the research data must contribute to understanding or insight about markets or customers that will underpin our decision making. Some surveys may provide direct feedback which can inform decisions quickly (such as product testing research), while other may provide context and long term value to how we define and interact with customers (e.g. audience segmentation).

Research should always focus on the overall objectives of the business or organisation; the information we collect should enable clear actions and underpin business decisions.

Market research in many ways is hard to define. Yes, all types of online surveys and market research generally, share a common thread: for example, the core objective of understanding audiences and their needs. Many online surveys will share common techniques and types of question styles. But beyond that, it is not possible to categorise every single type of research exercise. There are too many, and what researchers do evolves and is constantly changing.

Quantitative vs Qualitative Research

This chapter takes an overview of 10 of the most common types of market research undertaken online and using quantitative research techniques. In this book, I am focusing on quantitative research techniques rather than qualitative research. Qualitative research could easily be the subject of a whole book. I want to define it quickly, then move back to our core focus of online quantitative research.

Many people will be familiar with focus groups, used by political parties, to understand voter attitudes. They consist of a moderator, who asks questions to an audience of perhaps 6 or 8 individuals in a room. The questions are open ended, and the feedback is exploratory. The technique is in some ways akin to having conversations with people, and using the feedback of the conversations to analyse their responses. Focus groups are also increasingly undertaken online, because of the benefits of speed and cost - the same benefits as for online quantitative research! Qualitative researchers also engage with audiences via online bulletin boards and online communities. This is a very different discipline from quantitative research, which asks largely closed questions to larger representative samples. Qualitative research is arguably much better suited to exploring issues at an earlier stage of understanding about a market. It also has the benefit of examining issues in great detail and depth, as well as giving information in the respondents' own words as opposed to forcing the respondents to choose from limited question options.

 Qualitative research is characterised by open ended questions and is designed to explore issues.

Quantitative research asks largely closed questions to larger representative samples.

The tools and techniques of qualitative research are completely different to quantitative research. While online survey tools such as Surveygoo include open ended questions, the ability to conduct an online focus group, a bulletin board or run an online community is undertaken with different software, and online qualitative research is often practiced by specialist "qual researchers" or research agencies with core skills in qualitative research.

Qualitative research techniques, such as online focus groups or bulletin boards, tend to be undertaken by qualitative researchers with specialist software tools.

10 Popular Online Research Objectives

▶ Customer/Membership Satisfaction

▶ Customer Experience/Customer Journey

▶ Customer Service/Help Desk Performance

▶ Brand Awareness/Perceptions

▶ Pricing Research

▶ Audience/Market Segmentation

▶ Ad Testing

▶ Product Testing/New Product Development

▶ Audience Messaging

▶ Opinion Polls

Some agencies, for example, specialise in building bespoke online research communities for clients for a limited time or on an ongoing basis.

ℹ️ Online Research Community

Research communities are an alternative to open access online panels. They provide a forum for researchers to ask questions and run surveys (both qualitative and quantitative). They tend to be smaller and recruited from different sources, such as a customer database. They can take different forms, in terms of size, duration it operates and incentives. Membership is often private, based on invitation only.

It may well be that in the future client organisations start to use online qualitative research tools for themselves, but at the moment, DIY research is firmly associated with online quantitative surveys.

Customer or Membership Satisfaction

Customer satisfaction research explores what customers want from a provider, and how they perceive the provider. In practical terms online customer satisfaction surveys typically seek to understand how important given issues are and which are likely to contribute to an evaluation of a provider. The customer satisfaction survey usually measures the importance of supplier evaluation attributes, as well as the performance or rating of the same attributes. Customer satisfaction surveys of this kind have the benefit of providing key measures of performance, and can also be repeated, to provide tracking measures.

Membership satisfaction is a variation on customer satisfaction research. As the name suggests, the difference is the research measures the satisfaction of members (rather than customers). Arguably there are many similar issues between the two types of research. Membership bodies can be not for profit organisations, and typically provide unique services to their members which differentiates their service offering from other consumer or business facing organisations.

The terms customer satisfaction, and customer loyalty, are often used interchangeably, but they are different. A customer can be satisfied with a provider, and yet may still switch providers in the near future. Similarly, a customer may be very unsatisfied, but feel unwilling to switch provider in the near future for a number of reasons, including fear or poorer service from another supplier, or laziness! The point is, we should look to measure satisfaction and indictors of loyalty, and try to explore the complex relationship between satisfaction, loyalty, performance, context and brand.

One final variation on customer satisfaction which gained a lot of traction in recent years is the so called Net Promoter Score. The technique assess performance on a single metric (willingness to recommend) and categorises customers into three groups: Detractors, Passives and Promoters. The attraction of a simple way of measuring performance is easy to see, although, like most researchers I am sceptical of this technique as a replacement to deeper assessment of customer satisfaction and loyalty.

Customer Experience and Customer Journey

Customer experience research is a name given to research which looks to assess customer perceptions of the brand across multiple channels and events. It broadens the assessment from perhaps the narrower objectives performance and loyalty to perceptions of experiences and the brand.

A variation of customer experience is known as mapping the customer journey. Research can be conducted to measure perceptions at different points of engagement with the customer at different times. For example, a customer of a bank may interact with the bank online, on the telephone, in the branch and more broadly, as consumers of brand advertising or recipients of direct mail. Customer experience and journey research is a more complex set of activities, which is arguably best undertaken through a variety of research methods and separate activities. However, online research provides an opportunity to engage with customers at multiple points in the journey.

Customer Service and Help Desk Performance

Customer service research measures customer perceptions of functions associated with the support, customer service or help desk channels. Customer service research is typically undertaken close to the time of the point of interaction between the customer and the provider. For example, having had a telephone conversation with a customer services representative or spoken to a technical help desk, a short survey is sent to assess the satisfaction and outcome of the experience. Online research surveys are very well suited to customer service research objectives.

Brand Awareness and Perceptions

Brand awareness and perceptions research can easily be conducted online, and using quality online panels, allow the user to measure responses of a representative target audience. Brand awareness includes unprompted and prompted awareness as well as the extent to which the audience are familiar or knowledgeable about the product or brand. Typically this research can also measure product usage and brand loyalty. Brand perception research can be undertaken as part of a single awareness and perceptions measurement exercise, or, can be undertaken as a separate and more thorough exercise to explore how the brand is perceived, and specifically, which brand attributes it is associated with.

Pricing Research

Price is critical to any product or service, for both launching a new product or repositioning an existing offering. Pricing research is usually undertaken to ensure pricing is in line with market perceptions of value, to estimate the impact on sales if prices are modified, or to determine the relative value of product features against the price offering.

There are a number of ways to measure price perceptions. At the more complex end of possible techniques includes conjoint analysis and max-diff scaling. Conjoint analysis is based on the concept of customers trading off product features, including price. Although there are specialist tools to undertake conjoint surveys online, they are not simple to do, and it requires a reasonable level of knowledge to interpret the data.

However, there are other pricing research techniques which are simpler and within the capabilities of mainstream DIY online survey tools. For example, the Gabor Granger technique is widely applicable to different products and scenarios. The standard technique involves presenting a product and asking the probability of buying the product at a given price point. The data is easy to collect and relatively easy to collate and report.

A second method which is also relatively simple to script in an online survey is called the Price Sensitivity Measure (PSM). The technique involves probing the sensitivity range a respondent has towards a product idea, against a pre determined scale. It's advantage is that it allows a wider pricing scale and is well suited to measuring perceptions for new products, or products that are less well known. However, collating the data and reporting it is more difficult to achieve, although not impossible. It certainly doesn't require any specialist questionnaire design or analysis tools.

Audience/Market Segmentation

Marketers have long recognised that target markets and audiences are not a single, homogeneous entity. They consist of multiple groups and audiences, which need to be understood and communicated with appropriately.

Market segmentation research broadly has two objectives. Firstly, to identify groups or niches of people with common interests, needs, motivations and behaviour. Secondly, to understand how each group, or segment should be reached or engaged. Market segmentation research provides an essential route map for reaching out to markets, or audiences, from which relevant products, services or audience messaging can be successfully developed.

At the core of segmentation research is collecting attitudinal and behavioural data (e.g. attitudes to a product, preferences, personality, and consumption habits). While collecting this type of data is relatively easy (most online survey software have matrix and rating question types) it requires some knowledge to design relevant questions, as well as experience of appropriate multivariate analysis techniques (e.g. k means and cluster analysis).

Ad Testing

Online surveys are a very effective means to test consumer perceptions of adverts, including images and commercials. Ad testing tends to be undertaken at a relatively early stage in the creative process, to explore perceptions, and help steer the development of creatives. Mock up ads or storyboards can be developed in expensively and tested very quickly online. Ads can also be tested during or after the campaign as part of an evaluation of awareness of a campaign, and to explore its impact on brand perceptions. One of the key benefits of online panels is the ability to target very specific demographics. Combined with the fact that online surveys can be conducted very quickly, there has never been a better opportunity to conduct affordable and speedy research, at any time during the creative process, or as part of post campaign evaluations.

Product Testing and New Product Development

Product testing typically has four different objectives: test the viability of new products, or to assess perceptions of current product offerings; refine an existing offering or support the development of a new concept; estimate potential take up in the market; help define or adjust a pricing strategy. Research can provide an early steer on consumer needs as well as testing initial product ideas before reaching the stage of designing a full concept.

Again, online research is a fast and effective means of testing products, and given that research is capable of identifying clear product winners and losers, can be a very cost effective tool. Product testing online can be undertaken as a quantitative study as a single survey.

A variation on this is the so called In Home User Test (or sometimes called IHUT). Here, online panels are used to recruit relevant respondents to take part in a trial of a product, who are then required to provide feedback on the product over a set period of time, and potentially, to take answer several online surveys. Alternative methodologies include focus groups, bulletin boards, hall tests and traditional focus groups.

Audience Messaging

While Market Segmentation Research provides a framework for identifying audiences and understanding how to engage with them, Audience Message Testing is designed to explore and test message concepts and specific marketing messages.

Message Testing is relevant to marketeers who are looking to position a brand, new service and marketing campaign. It is also key to the objectives of ongoing and specific PR campaigns.

Market Research can assist in providing objective evidence of which messages are understood and valued, and how to refine messaging to make them effective and resonant with target audiences.

Audience Message Testing can be undertaken using both qualitative and quantitative research techniques.

Opinion Polls

Opinion polls are regularly used by PR Agencies and marketeers. In the PR industry polls can be used to identify a theme or a subject to gain publicity for a brand or an organisation. They can also be used to underpin specific campaign messages, from issues of public safety to campaigns reinforcing brand or product launches.

Many online consumer polls focus on public attitudes about a topic or identify consumer trends. Some polls are fun and light hearted, while others are more serious, addressing issues of public health or safety. Online surveys, online panels, and DIY survey tools now make it easier and more affordable to conduct polls.

But, relative ease and falling costs of surveys do no obviate core principles of sound online survey design. Whether the polls are at the lighter or more serious end of the spectrum, all polls need to be undertaken carefully with special attention to the representatives off the audience and objective questions if they are to be seen as credible.

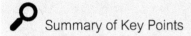 Summary of Key Points

Research should always focus on the overall business/organisation objectives; the information we collect should enable clear actions and underpin business decisions.

Qualitative research is characterised by open ended questions and is designed to explore issues. Quantitative research asks largely closed questions to larger representative samples.

Qualitative research techniques, such as online focus groups or bulletin boards, tend to be undertaken by qualitative researchers with specialist software tools.

Section 4
Create Your Online Survey

7: Planning your Survey

8: Question Types

9: Questionnaire Design

10: Scripting your Survey

This section covers the foundations of online research practice.

In chapter 7 we look at the key considerations for planning your project.

Chapter 8 provides an overview of common and new types of question types used in online surveys.

Chapter 9 takes a closer look at the core activity of questionnaire design, and finally, in chapter 10 we have a 'how to" guide on converting a draft questionnaire into a live online script, using the free online tool, Surveygoo.com.

Planning your Survey

"A goal without a plan is just a wish."

Antoine de Saint-Exupery

There are so many references in modern business practices about the need to plan. Yet many of us dislike the very idea of planning when we are busy or are working on competing priorities. If the task seems too small, there is a great temptation to drop any formal planning.

> But the truth is a plan does not need to be a long document, and however small the project, setting out a clear plan of action is a must.

For most organisations looking to commission research using an external consultant or market research agency, the internal stakeholders of the research will prepare some kind of market research brief. The research brief typically provides key background information about the organisation, the stakeholders, business challenges and the reason for conducting the research. It may also cover areas such as the likely methodology, objectives, timescales and deliverables. Consultants or market research agencies would then prepare a detailed proposal to address the requirements and priorities outlined in the research brief.

Each brief or project plan is different. It may be possible to prepare a plan in one page, or it may require 3 or 4. The length of the document is almost irrelevant. What is important is that we have a plan which ensures key issues around the research have been thought through.

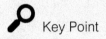 Key Point

Research consultants usually set out a clear proposal in response to a market research brief. Even if you are planning to undertake the survey in house, there is merit in preparing a suitable Research Plan as an essential part of the planning process.

Fashions in business change, as do practices. Fifteen years ago, the standard practice of researchers was to prepare lengthy proposals - 20 or more pages was the norm. Then increasingly it became more acceptable to prepare proposals as powerpoint slides, reducing the word count, and condensing the number of slides to as few as possible. In recent years it has been common to prepare simplified quotes rather than proposals. A former colleague of mine insisted on writing almost any proposal as a short email response. It may not have looked pretty, but in many cases it was certainly fit for purpose.

How you plan your research is up to you. But I would suggest that there are some key considerations which need to be addressed before pushing forward with the project. Here are a few example sub headings relevant to most research project plans.

Research Plan

- ☑ Background
- ☑ Business Objectives
- ☑ Methodology and Sampling
- ☑ Information Objectives
- ☑ Resources and Team
- ☑ Analysis Considerations and Deliverables
- ☑ Timescales

Background

A summary of the organisation and the situation currently faced, which provides context to why a research project is necessary. Clearly as an internal document, readers should know about the organisation. But if other individuals involved in the project are not close to a particular department, division, or team, it is essential that everybody involved has good background knowledge on who is commissioning the survey, who it is intended for and why research is being considered.

Business Objectives

Business or organisation objectives are not normally the same as information objectives, outlined below. The wider business objectives sets the scene as to what challenges are faced, and how research can help address those challenges. It should set out what can be achieved through research, and how research is to be used. For example, it could provide direct input into a key business decision, or it may provide market insight which will feed into another initiative. Being clear on what outcomes are required from the research because it will provide clarity as to what the research needs to achieve.

 Key Point

Business objectives are not the same as information objectives.

Methodology and Sampling

In most cases the methodology you will be considering internally will be an online survey using a survey tool. But we also need to be clear about the audience, sample size and the sample source. In turn we need to set out our requirements for sample quotas. For example, if we require a minimum or maximum number of completions of an age group or a customer of a particular brand.

Sample Source

The sample source is likely to be either an internal or bought in database, or an online access panel. The biggest question for many people is how large the sample size needs to be. There is no quick way to answer this, so let's go back to basics.

Sample Size

A sample is data which is representative of the total audience. In most cases, it's simply not practical (or possible) to survey the total audience or population. That would be a census. A sample is just part of the total population.

 Key Point

For most surveys we are aiming to achieve a representative sample of the population or business universe, as opposed to a census.

Lets say we want to find out what a representative sample of the UK population thinks about petrol prices in the UK. The sample is most likely to focus on drivers, although we may be interested in the total adult population. If we want the survey to be nationally representative, we will need a large sample. In the UK there are 12 Government regions, which are used to structure national samples. The table below shows the percentage (%) of the population accounted for in each region, and the number of respondents (N=) that would be provided in a nationally representative survey of 1,000 survey completions.

Region	%	N=
North East	4.3	43
North West	11.4	114
Yorkshire/ Humberside	8.5	85
East Midlands	7.1	71
West Midlands	9.0	90
East of England	9.1	91
Greater London	12.2	122
South East	13.7	137
South West	8.5	85
Scotland	8.7	87
Wales	5.2	52
Northern Ireland	2.8	28

When we are comparing groups of people (for sub groups we need a minimum of 50 - 100 in consumer surveys and 30 - 50 in business to business surveys. In other words, as long as there are at least 50 - 100 responses per region, it is reasonable to compare the result. Therefore, it is likely we will want a sample size of 1,000. This will be sufficient to compare regions, assuming we have interview completions spread approximately according to the table above.

In general a larger sample size is desirable, but it is not always necessary. If you need to run a nationally representative survey, and you have the budget, then 1,000 or 2,000 survey completions is advisable for a consumer survey. It can be overkill, though.

It is not the size of the audience which determines the sample size, but the minimum level of variation for the subgroups we can tolerate. We have already seen the example of a nationally representative survey by region above. But if wanted to survey just Mums with children between the ages of 5 and 12, a sample size of 200 - 400 may be sufficient, if we were not focused on regional differences, but were interested in splitting out key age groups of 5 - 8 and 9 - 12 (e.g. 100 or 200 in each age band).

Sample sizes for business to business surveys tend to be much smaller than consumer surveys. One reason is that business samples tend to be more homogeneous than is the case for consumer surveys. Finance Directors in large corporates tend to be relatively less diverse in opinion when talking about accounting software than say consumer preferences for holiday destinations. It's also true that the business "universe" is smaller.

i Nationally Representative Sample

A survey which is broadly representative of the national population in terms of age, gender and region. Sometimes called 'Nat rep" or 'Gen pop' (General population).

For example, the number of large companies (more than 1,000 employees in the UK) is fewer than 1,300 in 2008, according to the Office of National Statistics. Similarly, certain industry sectors may only have hundreds of companies. It is more likely that in business to business surveys, it is necessary to structure the sample by practical considerations. It may be possible to get 500 responses from HR managers across a broad range of business sizes and industry sectors. But if you are trying to size the potential market spend in the oil and gas sector, it may be necessary to aim for a near census of perhaps a few dozen companies.

 It is not the size of the audience which determines sample size, but the minimum level of variation for the sub groups we can tolerate.

Most of us are not trained statisticians. In fact, many people designing and using market research are not trained statisticians. Deciding the right sample size is also, in the real world, about balancing practical considerations of what is possible, affordable and credible. But using a few basic principles, most people are capable of arriving at an appropriate answer for planning a reasonable sample size.

Sample Quotas

If you have specific requirements for achieving a minimum, or maximum number of interviews in a particular demographic, you need to highlight the target. For example, if we only want respondents in the age groups 25-34 and 35-44 but want to exclude 17-24 and 65+. We may also want 60% of the responses to be women and 40% to be men.

Other Sampling Criteria

Apart from age, gender or region, it may be necessary to target an audience by other screening criteria. Some of the criteria could be captured as a profiled data point on an online panel (e.g. if we know a respondent is a driver, or consumes a stated amount of alcohol).

 Sample Quota

A method to ensure a set number of survey completions against set criteria, most commonly demographic (e.g. age and gender).

In other cases, we will need to ask one or several screening questions to make sure we are reaching the right type of respondent. It's not necessary, at this stage, to craft the questions but we do need to highlight any relevant screening criteria which will inform the person designing the questionnaire - even if that person is you!

Information Objectives

Information objectives are absolutely core to the planning process and the overall chances of the project delivering actionable outcomes. Put simply, information objectives are a list of subject or topic areas. They can also be prepared as a series of bulleted points. Think of information objectives as a summary list of information or feedback you want from the audience. It is not a questionnaire, but a statement of the information outcome you need.

 Being clear about the required information objectives is key to the success of a project. Put simply, they are a list of subject or topic areas to be covered in the research.

For example, a survey about brand perceptions may have half a dozen key information objectives: unprompted brand awareness, prompted brand awareness, brand usage, brand associations, brand satisfaction, brand loyalty, etc. The overall aims of the information objectives would be to provide an accurate measurement of brand perceptions about your brand, and key competitors. The detailed information objectives would be the specific pieces of information you are looking to collect, as part of the wider assessment of brand performance.

Resources and Team

You need to set out how much time you will need to execute the project, and identify the human and financial resources needed. It may be just yourself, or could involve several individuals, who could share responsibility for the project. For example, responsibilities for questionnaire design, survey scripting, checking questionnaires and scripts, securing a database, reviewing and reporting and presenting the results could be shared across several people in a team, or be undertaken by just one person responsible for the project.

Analysis Considerations and Deliverables

It is always a good idea to think about the deliverables from the start of a project. The core deliverables will be data tables and in all likelihood some kind of summary report. It may also be necessary to prepare a presentation for a single audience or different teams.

> Most survey tools like Surveygoo do much of the heavy lifting for you: data tables, a top line summary report, and the ability to run cross tabulations.

Having looked at these outputs, the hard bit is collating the data, interpreting and summarising the findings into a word or powerpoint report. If there are particular types of post survey analysis to be undertaken it is important to be clear about these from the outset. It's always possible to interrogate data in statistical packages like SPSS, but having a clear idea on the types of data analysis to be undertaken before you start the project will help.

For example, if a key aim of a survey is to establish demand for a new product and to assess price sensitivity, knowing what type of questioning technique and the expected analysis outputs would inform the questionnaire design process.

Of course, many surveys are relatively straightforward and do not require specialist question types. Even so, having a picture of the information objectives, and how you might present the results will help to ensure information objectives are met, and the survey results feed into actions.

Timescales

Every project plan should set out a clear timing plan. Allow enough time for each activity, and be realistic about possible delays if involving other team members in the project. The most common blockages in the execution of projects revolve around waiting on others! For example, delivering a database of contacts, writing an introduction email, agreeing project and information objectives, reviewing the draft questionnaire. Generally, the more people involved in the project, the greater the chances of delay. If there are key dates to be met (e.g. a date of a key meeting) put these in first, and then work backwards. Add your own key internal review dates, and be clear about who is responsible for a task and the date of the milestone (e.g. database to be supplied by a certain date, questionnaire review date, scripting final survey, etc).

Summary of Key Points

Research consultants usually set out a clear proposal in response to a market research brief. Even if you are planning to undertake the survey in house, there is merit in preparing a suitable Research Plan as an essential part of the planning process..

Business objectives are not the same as information objectives.

For most surveys we are aiming to achieve a representative sample of the population or business universe, as opposed to a census.

It is not the size of the audience which determines sample size, but the minimum level of variation for the sub groups we can tolerate

Being clear about the required information objectives is key to the success of a project. Put simply, they are a list of subject or topic areas to be covered in the research

Question Types Used in Online Surveys

Changing Methods, New Ways of Asking Questions

The tool kit of survey questions has grown significantly in the last few years with the appearance of more survey tools. In many ways online surveys provide new opportunities to ask questions in new ways. As market research has evolved, so has the way we ask questions.

When face to face interviews were the primary means for asking survey questions, the role of the interviewer was key. The interviewer was essentially the gatekeeper, responsible for delivering the questions to the respondent, and ensuring that the questions were understood, and properly collated without introducing bias in the data. The question sets which developed were designed to make that process smooth and practical. The same could be said of telephone interviewing.

With postal surveys, however, there was no gatekeeper to ensure the survey was completed properly. The postal questionnaire required the survey to be self completed by the respondent.

So it was now essential that the questionnaire was skillfully designed so that any respondent could understand the questions and could easily complete the questionnaire. At the same time, the questionnaire needed to be designed in such a way that it encouraged a good level of response: with no intervention from a skillful interviewer, the appearance and interest of the questionnaire was the only means to motivate respondents to answer the questions.

In this sense, the online survey has something in common with postal surveys. It is no surprise, then, that many of the question types and modes of asking online questions have a strong similarity with postal questionnaires.

 Question instructions, page layout, grid questions, tick box questions are all formats and considerations important to both postal and online questionnaires.

In fact, the early examples of online questionnaires were in many ways resembled postal questionnaires. It's not surprising because researchers spent years perfecting their techniques for asking self completion questions. The early online questionnaires were very basic in terms of look and the functionality was essentially an electronic version of a paper questionnaire. In fact, some of the early software packages enabled the design of questionnaires which could be delivered as both postal and online surveys.

Improving on Self Completion Questionnaires

Even the early versions of online surveys brought new opportunities to improve the quality of data collected by self completions means. Leaving aside presentation issues for the time being, there were a number of technical advantages. For example, the ability to randomise the order in which the response codes of questions appear, to bring forward answers given in previous questions to subsequent questions (often known as "piping"), to force respondents to answer a question before moving on to the next question, and the ability to direct respondents through to answer different questions or sections of a questionnaire based on their previous answers (often known as "routing" or "skip logic") were all innovations which were made possible by online surveys. Most of these features (and others) are often standard or accessible for a low cost with most web based survey tools.

 Entry or low cost online survey tools offer functions such as piping, randomisation, mandatory questions, and question routing, which are not possible in self administered paper questionnaires.

Understanding Basic and Advanced Question Types

If you are new to online surveys, or you have recently acquired a new online survey tool, one of the early tasks recommended, before designing a questionnaire is to familiarise yourself with the available question types.

The number of question styles is growing all the time, largely in response to the need to find new and more interesting ways to ask questions, which hold the respondent's interest and underpins better quality responses.

This chapter is concerned with the types of question format which are available in popular and affordable online survey tools. The process of selecting question types, and designing a questionnaire is discussed in chapter 9.

Closed Versus Open Questions

Earlier in chapter 6 we briefly covered the difference between qualitative and quantitative research. In a similar way we can easily differentiate question types between open ended and closed questions. That is, the difference between open and closed questions is equally fundamental. Essentially, all questions are usually either an open or a closed question. Open questions ask a question and provide a space for the answer, in which the respondent writes in the answers. Most other types of question style are closed questions. The distinguishing characteristic of open ended questions is that they elicit an unprompted response, which gives the respondent free reign in making their response. It can result in very rich data, as well as the opposite - a poor quality response. The key disadvantage, however, is that they are difficult to analyse and quantify (more on open ended questions below).

Question types are either open or closed. An open question allows the respondent to write in their answer in free form; a closed question presents a fixed range of options for the respondent to choose from.

Closed questions are, by definition, a question type which presents a set of options, which closes down the range of responses to a pre-determined list.

There are several advantages associated with closed questions. First, the fact that questions display a list of answer codes makes it a simple process of completing the question. Some closed questions are more difficult to fill in than others (e.g. long matrix questions) but in general, they are an easy option for the survey participant. Second, because the respondent merely has to read through the list of options, rather than write in answers (as with open ended questions), they are often quick to fill out. The third advantage is perhaps the most significant and is particularly important from the point of view of the user of the research. Closed questions automatically codify the data we collect. When it comes to analysing the responses, the data is automatically tabulated which is a huge time saver.

Closed questions also have disadvantages: namely that they limit the number of answers, do not allow respondents to freely express their answers, and in broader terms are less useful for exploratory data (see chapter 6: differences between quantitative and qualitative research).

Closed questions automatically codify the data we collect. When it comes to analysing the responses, the data is automatically tabulated. This a a huge time saver.

Classification, Demographics and Screener Questions

Before considering the common and lesser known question types, we should begin with questions which either are designed to classify responses for analysis purposes, or to determine the eligibility of respondents to answer a full questionnaire.

Demographic questions, as the name suggests, categorises respondents by their demographic profile, most commonly, age, gender and region. These questions are typically asked before the main questions, so that demographic questions can be used to screen-out respondents. For example, if we only wanted women between the age of 18-24 to answer the survey, a gender and age question, would allow us to capture relevant respondents to go through the questionnaire. If a survey was relevant to all demographics, you could choose to ask demographic questions at the back of the questionnaire. In Surveygoo, for example, there are pre-set demographic questions which appear at the beginning of the questionnaire.

Classification questions are similar to demographic questions, insofar as they are typical questions to capture "categorical' data. They can also be used to set sample quotas and to screen-out respondents. For example, classification questions could include income level, education level, household income, and household size. In business to business surveys, classification questions might include industry sector, size of organisation, job function and other activity related criteria (e.g. propensity to use a particular service or product).

Screener questions vary considerably because they are often related to the subject. For example, we might only want to interview very active users in Facebook, or people who used a combination of Facebook and Twitter on a regular basis. A screener question would capture which respondents were active users, as defined by the question, and would screen out those respondents who did not qualify. In more complex audience targeting, there could be a series of screener questions to arrive at the appropriate target audience.

Demographic questions categorises respondents by their demographic profile, most commonly, age, gender and region. Classification questions also group respondents which can be used to set quotas, such as household income or industry sector. Screener questions are used to qualify respondents for their eligibility to answer a survey, based on qualifying criteria.

Core Question Types

☑ Single or Multiple Choice (Choice questions)

☑ Drop Down Questions

☑ Matrix (Grid) Questions

☑ Open Ended Questions

Lets start with the most common question types, familiar to survey respondents and widely used in online surveys.

Single Choice and Multiple Questions

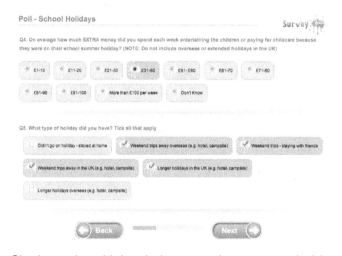

Single and multiple choice questions are probably the most common type of question style, used to varying degrees in surveys. They are simple to create, do not take long to complete, and have the advantage of being readily understood by survey participants. They can appear as a dichotomous question (e.g. yes/no answers) or more typically, as longer lists of answers. As the name suggests, a single choice question requires the respondent to select just one answer, and a multiple choice question allows the respondent to select multiple answers. A variation on the multiple choice question is the ability to set the maximum number of answers which can be selected. For example, ask the respondent to select up to three items from a list of 10. Different online survey tools have different names for most question types. The technical name for a single choice question with a scale is "single question scalar response". Surveygoo calls the single and multiple questions a Choice question.

Drop Down Questions

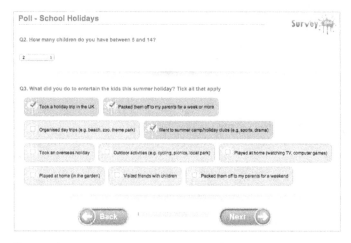

Drop down questions are also widely used and are perfect for a single code questions with a limited number options. Again, it will be a question type which will feel familiar and easy to complete to respondents (its the kind of thing we see in website forms), but also, it has the benefit of fitting neatly in a small space on a questionnaire page. Drop downs can be written as a scale, or a non scale question, which can also be randomised. To some extent they accommodate longer code frames (number of response options) and can still fit easily in the page. Arguably, these are also reasonably engaging, insofar as they encourage the respondent to click on the question to see all the answers.

Matrix (Grid) Questions

Q2. When choosing a PR agency, what is most important to you?

	Critical	Very Important	Quite important	Not very important	Not at all import
Creative thinking	○	○	⊙	○	○
Track record - in my industry	○	○	⊙	○	○
Knowledge of market issues in my sector	○	○	⊙	○	○
Quality of team	○	○	⊙	○	○
Competitive price	○	○	⊙	○	○
Expertise in digital communications	○	○	⊙	○	○
Reputation	○	○	⊙	○	○
International reach	○	○	⊙	○	○
Global agency	○	○	⊙	○	○

Matrix questions, or grid questions as they are often called, are a very versatile question style and widely used. They are efficient in the sense they can capture several columns of data in the same question. For example, show several brands and collect responses to multiple attributes, as in the example below.

The versatility leads to matrix questions being used widely: rating, importance measurement, any any scaled questions with multiple question attributes. If used sparingly, they are a very useful question type. Because they are used widely, they are familiar to respondents. But the problem with matrix questions is the temptation to load up the question with too many question codes/attributes or scales/data columns. Long, complex matrix questions can be off putting to the respondent and it is sometimes argued, encourages the respondent to answer the question too quickly - by having the same answer response in the column. This is known among researchers as "straight-lining". Of course, respondents who are not interested in giving considered answers and taking the appropriate time to read questions, are likely to complete all questions in the same way. But at the same time, it is fair to say that overly long, complex matrix questions, increase the likelihood of poor quality responses. There is nothing worse than page after page of long matrix questions. It's enough to kill interest in any survey. That is not to say that matrix questions do not have a use - they do - but we should be careful when using them.

Open Ended Questions

Open ended questions are frequently used in online surveys but tend to be used sparingly in each survey, mostly because the data is hard to analyse, as we discussed above. In some ways breaking up closed questions with the occasional open ended question can help add some variety to questionnaires; they can also complement closed questions by exploring an issue or set of issues touched on previously with closed questions. For example, to ask why an answer was given in a previous question.

Broadly, open ended questions typically appear in three variations: a) open ended text box b) single code box c) multiple text boxes. The Open ended text box style is designed to make room for a longer response - a paragraph of text. The way the text box often appears on the survey (a larger stretched area text box) signals to the respondent that they should write a longer answer of sentences or multiple ideas. This has the benefit of encouraging rich data, but is harder to analyse.

The single open ended text box also allows the respondent to write in words, but since it appears as a small box, invites the respondent to write fewer words. It is typically suited to recording brands or concepts which can be summarised in a single word or a few words. In Surveygoo, the single open ended question can also be used to capture numerical data instead of text data. The numerical data is, by contrast, coded and easily reported in the data tables.

The third variation of open ended questions, the multiple open ended question, is useful for capturing open ended lists, or open ended ordered lists. For example, which brands come to mind, or list in order of priority the three factors most important when assessing a brand.

The format of several separate text boxes encourages the respondent to separate out their responses. Again, it's better suited to teasing out single issues or simple sentences rather than paragraphs. It is also relatively easier to analyse than the open end question which captures a paragraph of text.

Questions for Testing Ads

- ☑ Static image questions

- ☑ Video and moving image questions

Image Questions

Online surveys are a very good medium for testing audience perceptions of creatives, such as logos and still image adverts. Many survey tools make the process of testing creatives very easy: upload the image and insert the question. An image could be loaded, followed by several questions; in other cases, several images are tested alongside each other. In Surveygoo, for example, image questions can be tested as an open ended question as well as a choice question (single/multi-code question).

Video Questions

A variation on Image Questions is the Video Question. As the name suggests, the purpose is to test a video rather than a still image. It's perfect for testing adverts. Again, most survey tools make it easy to upload a video directly into the questionnaire.

Questions to Engage

- ☑ Ranking Questions

- ☑ Drag and Drop Questions

- ☑ Slider Questions

Researchers are increasingly concerned that online surveys do a better job of engaging with respondents. The look and feel of survey questions, the question types used, as well as the wording of questions have an impact on how respondents perceive and participate in surveys. Survey tool providers are looking at new ways to ask questions. Recent examples of more interactive questions include drag and drop questions, sliders, star rating questions and card sort questions.

Ranking Question

The older method for obtaining ranking data (e.g. rank the importance of the following factors) was to use a grid or matrix style question. A variation on the ranking question is the use of drag and drop features: the respondent drags the items in the question into a box and then reorders the items, again by dragging them.

As we have already discussed, grid questions can appear to be complex, and can lead to a poorer quality of response from survey participants. A ranking question which makes use of drag and drop effects is more intuitive and is considered to improve respondent engagement.

The main advantage of ranking questions is that they force the respondent to make a clear choice between the attributes presented. This can be particularly useful when it is necessary to prioritise issues (e.g. new product features on a software product most required, or in polling surveys where the researcher may be hoping for some distinctive results). However, by the same token it can be argued that in circumstances where a respondent would more realistically place a multiple of attributes at a similar level of importance, the ranking question is less useful (e.g. a ranking question provides a unique rank for each attribute, but does not allow a shared ranking of more than one attribute).

The other issue with ranking questions, in the context of respondent experience, is limitation on the number of attributes. If there are only a few attributes in the ranking question (e.g. 5 to 7) they are relatively fast to complete, but beyond 8 - 10 attributes, they can become complicated and time consuming for the survey participant.

Drag and Drop Question

There are several types of Drag and Drop question types. They include any question where the respondent is required to move an object (graphic or text) to a box or area of a question in order to complete the question.

For example, drag and drop can include ranking questions (as above) as well as dragging images, words or points on a scale. In Survegoo the standard Drag and Drop question is a variation of a matrix/grid question. But instead of clicking on a point on a grid, the respondent drags a circle into a cell, within a grid. A multi-code drag and drop works on the same principle but features tick marks in post it note style, which again needs to be dragged into the appropriate cell.

Slider Questions

Q7. Which of the following potential benefits of DIY research do you agree with. Use the slider below to indicate how much you agree each is a benefit of DIY research. 0 = No Benefit 100=Significant Benefit

Staff know more about its own products/customers/markets 35

Significant cost savings (no external consultant costs) 35

Better control over project design/execution 35

Fast - quicker to plan and implement 35

Generates more internal 35

Makes budgets go further 35

Good option for less important / less strategic research 35

There are a number of variations on slider questions, but the general principle of sliders is that the respondent uses a slider graphic, and drags along a marker to a point on a graphical scale (usually a line).

Different survey tools have variations on sliders, but most allow the scale to be changed and to set the interval points. Sliders have the benefit of being interactive and encourage the respondent to engage with the question, and, when it is possible to change the scale, is a versatile question style.

Other Question Types

- ☑ Star Rating Questions
- ☑ Emoticons Questions
- ☑ Card Sort Questions
- ☑ Constant Sum Scale
- ☑ Rich Text

Star Rating Question

There are too many new and emerging question types to keep track of them all. Most new types are a variation of drag and drop. For example, a Star rating question shows a series of attributes in a grid, but instead of a matrix or slider scale, are star graphics. The respondent clicks on the number of stars for the attribute. It is a simple and quite flexible question style which can be adapted to different scaler uses. The number of stars (usually up to 5) becomes the scale. So for example, questions like "how do you rate" and "how much do you like" would not have a named scale, but would be represented by star symbols.

Emoticons

A variation on Star questions are so called emoticons. These type of question can feature a graphic such as a "smiley face" or other clip art style graphics which may be interactive or static. An interactive version would allow the respondent to click and change a scale on the graphic which will then either show the scale as a number or a change to the graphic (such as a deeper smile, or unhappy face). In other examples, such as Surveygoo's Emoticon, the graphic of a smiley face is a series of static images.

Card Sort Question

Card or graphic sort questions allow the user to drag an image or text into groups of boxes or categories. It's a versatile question style and is a potential replacement to the grid question style. Whereas a traditional grid presents all the options at the same time, a Card Sort question presents each question attribute one at a time. This forces the respondent to concentrate and focus on answering one question at a time. It is more interactive, and the evidence suggests that the temptation to "straight-line" answers is reduced.

Constant Sum Scale

A Constant Sum Scale question asks the respondent to allocate points across a number of factors or attributes, up to total number of points. It's an old technique which is often under used. The main benefit of the constant sum scale technique is that it enables respondents to express relative interest across factors by allocating points across the factors. They effectively "trade off" the points (e.g. if you have above average points for some factors, the remaining factors must have less than average, in order for the points to add up to the total).

In Surveygoo, this question type is called a Sum Scale, and is an interactive question, insofar as the respondent must drag on a scale to activate the points, and it shows a running total of the points allocated.

Rich Text

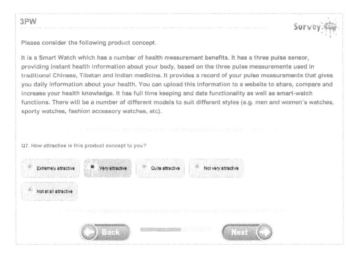

Rich Text questions are not technically a question at all. They are a place to provide text or paragraph of explanation in between questions, to pre-warn and provide guidance before questions are shown.

Summary: Comparison of Question Types

In chapter 9 we will look at how different question types can be applied to different research and information objectives. In most surveys it is normal to have a mix of question styles, and the balance of questions used will be related to the objectives of the survey.

From the perspective of how the survey respondent interacts with questions, we can differentiate four factors, which could influence the selection of question styles. These factors are not scientifically tested and do not have a comparative, intrinsic value.

But from a practical viewpoint they are valid. First, the extent to which the question type is intuitive for the respondent. In essence, is the question something the respondent feels they can engage with and know how to use it. Second, is how easy the question is to complete. Third, engagement refers to the extent to which the question will engage and motivate the respondent. Lastly, versatility refers to the ability to use the question type for different purposes and information objectives.

The following table summarises the differences between the main question types against these four factors. For example, the newer question types such as drag and drop, score higher on engagement although not necessarily the highest on Intuitiveness. Matrix and Matrix ranking questions score relatively lower on all factors.

Question Type	Intuitive	Ease of use	
Choice	High	High	
Drop Down	High	High	
Matrix	Low	Low	
Open Ended	Medium	Low	
Image/ Video	High	High	
Ranking (matrix)	Low	Low	
Ranking (drag and drop)	Medium	Medium	
Drag and Drop	Medium	High	
Slider	Medium	High	
Star Rating	Medium	High	
Emoticons	High	High	
Card Sort	High	High	
Constant Sum Scale	Low	Medium	

Engagement	Versatility
Medium	Medium
Medium	Low
Low	Medium
Medium	Low
High	Low
Low	Medium
High	Medium
High	High
High	Medium
Medium	Medium
High	Medium
High	High
Medium	Low

Summary of Key Points

Question instructions, page layout, grid questions, tick box questions are all formats and considerations important to both postal and online questionnaires.

Entry or low cost online survey tools offer functions such as piping, randomisation, mandatory questions, and question routing, which are not possible in self administered paper questionnaires.

Question types are either open or closed. An open question allows the respondent to write in their answer in free form; a closed question presents a fixed range of options for the respondent to choose from.

Closed questions automatically codify the data we collect. When it comes to analysing the responses, the data is automatically tabulated. This a a huge time saver.

Demographic questions categorises respondents by their demographic profile, most commonly, age, gender and region. Classification questions also group respondents which can be used to set quotas, such as household income or industry sector. Screener questions are used to qualify respondents for their eligibility to answer a survey, based on qualifying criteria.

Suggested Follow Up Exercises

Refer to the Quick Guide: Surveygoo Question Types.

Use the free templates available (Customer Satisfaction or Employee Satisfaction) to set up and preview a survey

Set up a new questionnaire and experiment with all types of question style available

Designing
Questionnaires

"Design is a mix of craft, science, storytelling, propaganda and philosophy"

Erik Adigard

Honing your questionnaire design skills will take time and practice. As you get used to designing a few different types of questionnaire, you will become familiar with the common question types, and become quicker at the task. The best way of learning is trial and error. Don't expect your early efforts to be perfect, and be prepared to learn from the experience. For example, you will start to see which types of questions and question wording tends to elicit a better response.

> Of course you can read around the subject and follow examples, but in reality, only by seeing mistakes at first hand can you recognise what works best, less well and what mistakes should be avoided at all costs.

Of course, many readers of this book are not aiming to become an experienced market researcher or an expert in questionnaire design, but may have the more modest ambition of wanting to get in a position of designing competent surveys for the occasions they need them. This chapter sets out the key lessons of questionnaire design, and how to avoid obvious mistakes. Nothing can replace practice and experience, but at the same time, being aware of rookie mistakes will help you save time and reduce the chances of designing poor surveys.

By definition, perfection is rarely obtainable. I often see surveys undertaken on online panels which I can't resist criticising (although not publicly!). Questionnaires can seem overly long, use confusing language, feature too many complex grid questions, look repetitive or boring.

Questionnaire design is a bit like language translations. In my experience of working with translators, a language translation is never perfect. You can easily go through reviews and multiple iterations of a translation with different reviewers identifying different issues or imperfections. The point is not to aim for perfection in design, style and tone. That is subjective and near impossible.

But to ensure a questionnaire is fit for purpose: that it observes basic guidelines around providing clear and unambiguous questions, which elicits reliable data. In truth, that is the best anyone can achieve, however experienced you are at questionnaire design.

 Good questionnaire design comes with practice. The aim is not perfection, but to design surveys which have clear an unambiguous questions.

Avoiding 15 Common Mistakes of Questionnaire Design

Before we look at the process and steps to designing a questionnaire, we will start with the common mistakes to avoid. Why 15? Yes, there are probably many more. These aren't by any means the full list and they are not shown in any particular order, but are a fair representation of the usual suspects.

1. Leading Questions

This is one of the most common mistakes. In some cases leading questions are written unintentionally. Here is an example. "Q. Do you agree with most people that the National Health Service is under funded?". The question wording is encouraging the respondent to say "Yes". It would be better to include the question within a set of statements in a matrix, and of course, to be neutral in the phrasing of the question. e.g. "Q. To what extent do you agree or disagree with the following statement... The NHS is underfunded."

In some cases individuals deliberately bias or force questions to get the "right" answers. For example, limiting the range of answers which can be given, excluding don't knows, as well as leading language. This should be avoided if you have any ambition to develop an objective questionnaire, which collects accurate feedback and can be seen to be credible.

2. Overly Complex Matrix Questions

This is a particular bug bear of mine. Too many questionnaires include page after page of long and complex matrix (grid questions). It may seem an efficient way to ask questions, but think about how the respondent will see the question. Respondent experience is key to the success of the questionnaire.

3. Confusing, Complex or Ambiguous Question wording

Take time to design questions which communicate the question simply while being objective. We are striving for simplicity and clarity. Using question instructions are a good way of ensuring the respondent knows how to answer the question. e.g. the instruction "Please tick all that apply" for a multiple choice question. Also, where possible, avoid jargon, technical phrases or colloquial expressions which may not be understood by the audience.

4. Imprecise Questions

Precision and ambiguity are related. If you ask the question, "Q. Have you been to the pub recently" it is likely to be interpreted differently by respondents (e.g. what does recent mean) and lead to inconsistent interpretation and, therefore, inaccurate responses. But asking, "Q. Have you been to the pub in the last week", is clear and precise. Similarly, for open ended questions we need to be careful to use precise language which does not give too much latitude for the respondent to give a wide range of answers. For example, "Q. What suggestions do you have for improving canned tomatoes?" is very open; using the wording "Q. What suggestions do you have for improving the taste of canned tomatoes" narrows the response down. Open ended questions are used to get open feedback, but be careful not to make them too open. So be precise.

5. Double Questions

Sometimes there is a temptation to combine two questions in one. e.g. "Q. Do you think taxes are too high and complicated?" Don't do this. Always ensure there is a single, clear purpose to the question.

6. Too many open ended questions

Open ended questions are a valuable question type, but they should not be used as a substitute to taking the time to develop a meaningful set of answer codes for a closed question. Open ended questions are more difficult to analyse, and although when used sparingly, they can elicit a good level of response, using too many is likely to result in respondent fatigue and a poor quality of response.

7. Mixed rating scales

It is often not practical to feature exactly the same question scales throughout all questions. In fact, using very similar questions can look repetitive and confusing. On the other hand, featuring scaled questions which have a wide range of scales and are constantly changing (e.g. 3 point, 5 point, 7 point, verbal, etc) can also be confusing.

8. Innacurate Answers

Do not ask for precise numerical data when the precise answer is likely to be inaccurate or hard to estimate. For example, "Q. How much have you spent on lunches this month?". The question forces the respondent to calculate the answer quickly and probably inaccurately. It would be better to ask "Q. How much did you spend on lunches last week (Monday - Friday) and present answer options in ranges. Having done the survey, you can "gross up" the answer (e.g. multiply the average answer by 4 weeks), to arrive at an average value for a month. Alternatively, use answer codes to represent likely values in answer bands. In general answers should typically fall within the middle of a range.

By contrast, asking how old the respondent is can be asked as a open ended numerical question without fear of the respondent not being able to give a precise answer.

9. Poor Question Sequence

It is often recommended to ask easier questions earlier in the questionnaire, to encourage the respondent to answer the survey. The idea is that the respondent would be put off by complicated questions early on in the survey. Arguably, sequencing by topic area is more important. Make sure that the questions are rolled out in sequence e.g. topic areas a grouped together in logical sections.

10. Complex question routing

Question routing is used to ensure that relevant questions are asked to respondents based on their previous answers. There is no point in asking a set of questions to a respondent about their experience of business travel if the respondent has already indicated earlier in the questionnaire that they do not travel overseas on business.

Be clear about how key questions can be used to guide the respondent through the questionnaire without forcing them to answer inappropriate questions. Keep routing as simple as possible - the more complex it is the greater the chance that you will fail to pick up a routing error when you are scripting the questionnaire. Also, complex routing which reduces the sample base unnecessarily is pointless e.g. if the number of people relevant to answer sections of the questionnaire is too small to make the answers meaningful.

11. Negative Wording

Try to avoid questions where double negatives can confuse the required answer. For example, "Q. Are you against a ban on Fox hunting". The meaning of the question can be worked out, but at first glance the respondent may be confused which way to read and answer the question. "Do you agree, or disagree, that Fox Hunting should be banned?" might be longer winded, but it clearer.

12. Incomplete Answer Lists

When using pre-coded answer lists in multiple choice or grid questions, make sure you cover all the obvious and logical answers. If they are excluded, then the results will not be accurate. Of course, it is often not possible to identify all relevant answer codes, particularly if you are new to a subject or market. In which case conducting some qualitative research before hand may be necessary, or at the very least a pilot survey which includes some open questions to identify relevant answers. But in all circumstances the range of answer options should address obvious, logical options.

13. Mutually Exclusive Answers

Make sure that you use answer responses (particularly in Single Choice questions) which are mutually exclusive, so that respondents can make clear choices. Non exclusive answers are inaccurate and frustrating for the respondent. You need to make sure the scale takes account of different opinions or behaviours so that each option is exclusive. For example, recording an age group where the age bands overlap (35 - 45 and 45 - 55) overlaps as opposed to 35 - 44 and 45 - 54, which does not).

14. Unbalanced Scales

There are times when using an unbalanced rating scale is useful. For example, a customer survey where you are more interested in differentiating levels of excellence. In which case, a scale of Excellent, Very good, good, fair, poor, would be appropriate. But if the aim is to get an accurate measure of a medical condition, we need to take care that we accurately record the range. e.g. alcohol units consumed recorded in equal ranges, to reflect all levels of likely consumption.

15. Inappropriate Page Layout

This is a common mistake and comes with practice. It is not a good idea to feature too many questions on the same page. There is no absolute maximum or minimum, and it also depends on the length of the questions. Use your common sense. Having a single page of 10 or 15 questions is not recommended. There are times, when a short form-like questionnaire can be combined on a single page, but in most cases, questionnaires should be spread out over multiple pages. There is a case to be made for having no more than 2 to 3 questions on a page, and some researchers prefer to have a single question per page so that the respondent can concentrate on one question at a time.

Five Key Stages of Questionnaire Design

☑ Survey Plan

☑ Questionnaire Plan

☑ Select Questions

☑ Write Questionnaire

☑ Review

Step 1: Have a Survey Plan

It sounds obvious, but if you rush into a questionnaire without taking the time to think about the wider aspects of the survey objectives and how to implement it, there is a greater chance the end result will not work as well as it could, or in extreme cases, will be a failure.

Be clear about the survey objectives, the sample size, sample source, sample quotas, screening and targeting respondents (and on what criteria), key information objectives, and analysis considerations. These will all have an impact on how a questionnaire is approached and implemented. Chapter 7 outlined the practical considerations of Planning a Survey.

Be clear about your Survey Plan before starting to design the questionnaire.

Step 2: Plan the Questionnaire

Just as it is recommended to have a Survey Plan (even if it is a basic outline), it is also recommended that you plan out your questionnaire (Questionnaire Plan) before committing to designing the questionnaire. In my view, even a relatively short or simple survey, can benefit from a questionnaire plan. What information are you looking to get back from the survey? What types of question and question answer is appropriate to meet those objectives.

 Plan out the contents, topics and structure of the questionnaire before writing the detailed questions and designing the questionnaire.

Next, map out the subject areas or possible sub sections within the questionnaire. Always prioritise the key information objectives to avoid asking "nice to know" or time-wasting questions. At this point we are not scripting detailed and refined questions, but general question objectives and question areas.

Lastly, map out the rough order of questions and overall flow of the questionnaire. Much of this is about logic and common sense. For example, if an important element of the survey objectives is to measure unprompted awareness, make sure the respondents see unprompted questions in the question sequence before prompted lists of brands, which would bias the results.

Make sure the sequence of questions matches the natural order in which a set of topics should unfold. In general screening questions (designed to identify those respondents relevant to answer the questionnaire) should be at the front and any key demographic questions. If you have sensitive questions, it is a good idea to ask them later on in the questionnaire rather than upfront, although it is reasonable to pre warn respondents about the subject matter if it is particularly sensitive.

While some demographic questions which are relevant to setting screening criteria and sample quotas should be at the front of the survey, other more detailed classification information could be placed at the end of the questionnaire.

Step 3: Review and Select Question Types

There are many types of questions which can be asked with online surveys. Ideally you should be aware of the full range of question types provided in specific survey packages. Chapter 8 provided a review of the more common types and less common survey questions. Survey tools like Surveygoo also provide ready-to-go survey templates which can be useful for getting an idea of how questions can used in a specific context (e.g. common question styles used in employee satisfaction, or website feedback surveys).

The following key question types are used in a specific context.

- ☑ open or closed questions

- ☑ single or multiple choice

- ☑ spontaneous or prompted

- ☑ open ended or pre-coded answer options

- ☑ ranking questions

Open questions may include a code frame. e.g. Why did you buy a brand of toothpaste (with options displayed). But pre-coded closed questions may present a list and direct the respondent to select one or a finite number of options from the list. The simplest closed question is called a dichotomous question, I.e. a response where a yes or no is required.

 Familiarise yourself with the types of questions available in a survey package and look at ready-made-templates available in survey tools before designing a questionnaire.

Multiple choice questions present a list and ask the respondent to select several options. This is commonly used for brand awareness and usage questions. e.g. Which of the following brands do you know, have you purchased?

Uses of spontaneous questions include brand awareness, recall of adverts, attitudes to a product or concept. Uses of open ended questions include descriptions of a brand or product, reasons why an option of behaviour is given or improvements the customer would like to see.

Ranking questions are often used to rank product features, frequency of using something, or brand associations.

Step 4: Writing the Questionnaire

Once you are clear about the objectives, topics, audience, targeting, overall flow of the questionnaire and question types you should be ready to start designing the questionnaire. A key issue is whether you should design the survey in a word processor or paper first, or jump in an start scripting in the survey tool.

Part of the answer is how confident you are working straight in the tool, and the complexity of the questionnaire. Some survey packages allow you to export your scripted questionnaire so that you can review it offline. Overall , there is a strong case for designing the questionnaire in a word processor first. You can work on the question wording, amend, play with the order of questions, plan question routing until it is in a near final state.

In general, it is usually easier to design a questionnaire in a word processor before scripting it in a survey tool. It's easier to make changes and review early drafts of a questionnaire before it is scripted in the survey tool.

It is usually easier to share a draft questionnaire for review before scripting it. If a questionnaire is in a very draft format, it is often more difficult to make significant amendments within the scripting tool; it can be done but is likely to increase the chances of mistakes. Most online survey scripting companies ask their clients to provide a final questionnaire before scripting it; you should ask the same for your internal clients.

There are a number of considerations for writing the questionnaire, many of which we have touched on in the common mistakes section of this chapter.

On a broader level we need to be concerned with the general approach to writing the questionnaire. Here are some common themes and rules which should be applied to questionnaire design.

Language

Language and tone are critical for any questionnaire. Respondents need to understand the questions clearly and without ambiguity. At the same time they need to be comfortable with and sympathetic to the questions. The question topics and language must always be appropriate to the audience.

Use of Answer Codes

Getting the right pre-coded answer codes in place is critical. They need to be comprehensive, precise, meaningful and mutually exclusive.

Minimise Bias

Avoid using leading questions or double questions. Also, make sure that you consider question order where it can have an impact on bias (e.g. asking prompted questions before spontaneous questions). Use the randomise question answer function, so that respondents see the order of answers randomly.

Scales

Do not vary scales too much. Consider whether the scale should be balanced or unbalanced, and the number of intervals in the scale (5, 7, 10). Scales can have numbers in a logical order, or can be verbal.

Keep it simple

There are no special prizes for using more complex questions, language, code frames or routing then is necessary. I still have a lot of sympathy with the American acronym, the "K-I-S-S" approach. K-I-S-S is apparently derived from the US Navy in the 1960s, which set out simple processes of design to remove unnecessary complexity.

Questionnaire Length

There is no magic number of questions or length of interview, but in general terms long questionnaires risk poorer quality data. As a very rough rule of thumb 20 - 25 questions is a good number for a longish questionnaire. Well designed questionnaires which vary types of questions, are easily understood and where the subject matter is interesting, can support longer questionnaires. If you have a lot of survey objectives, consider splitting the survey into several different surveys.

Appealing Design

Try to remember how the questionnaire will look to the respondent. Make use of engaging question styles like sliders and drag and drop questions, and be aware of good page layout (e.g. do not put too many questions on a page). Some survey tools, including Survegoo, have a number of design themes which are fun, bold and interesting to the respondent which can improve engagement and response levels.

Step 5: Review, Test and Pilot the Questionnaire

Spend as much time as possible to check the questionnaire before attempting to script or launch the survey. In most cases the first draft of a questionnaire will have a few errors, and often final reviews of the questions will yield last minute ideas and improvements.

As you script your questionnaire you can preview the questionnaire, to make sure they look as they should.

Scripting

The word scripting refers to creating a working online survey in a survey tool of the questionnaire. It is sometimes used interchangeably with the word programming.

Its up to you if you preview while you set up a questionnaire, or wait until the end. Apart from using a preview function of the questionnaire before launching the survey (many survey packages allow this) it is also worth launching a test survey, and sharing it with one or two colleagues, to test the survey in a live environment. Once you are happy that it works as you intended and delivers the kind of live experience you feel is appropriate, you will have the confidence to launch it as a live survey.

We will look at the process of scripting a survey in more detail using Surveygoo as an example in the next chapter, including previewing and testing questionnaire scripts.

Professional market researchers often pilot surveys. Piloting is effectively a small scale version of the final version in order to do a thorough check of the questionnaire, and that it provides the type of results required. The decision to pilot a survey is partly down to time and money.

A variant of a pilot survey is a pre-test survey where a cut down version of the full survey is run to sanity check assumptions about the audience. e.g. what incidence of the population have used a certain product or are relevant to answer a full survey, and to test some key assumptions. The results of a pre-test may significantly alter the direction, approach or objectives of a main stage or subsequent surveys.

New Ways of Asking Old Questions

I have made repeated references throughout this book to the ongoing efforts for researchers to find new ways to make questions and questionnaires both more appealing and engaging to respondents. There is much evidence to support the view that engaged respondents are much more likely to provide better quality feedback.

The converse is true. Bored respondents provide bad data. In a research paper delivered by Deb Sleep from Engage Research, at a Market Research Society Conference on online research, evidence was presented showing the disruptive effect of bored respondents on survey data. The research indicated that bored respondents spent 17% less time answering questions, provided 41% fewer words in open ended questions, and there was a 38% increase in the tendency to "straight-line" or give pattern answers. There are numerous other studies from leading practitioners of online research who point to the same general conclusions: questionnaires need to engage respondents.

> Questionnaires which engage respondents results in better quality data. Questionnaires which bore respondents results in poor quality which can lead to wrong conclusions.

We have already touched on the efforts of software developers to create new and engaging question styles, and to design attractive questionnaires, such as survey themes and graphics. But there are other small, practical steps the researcher can take to improve the level of response from the questions we ask based on how we word the questions.

From Personal to Projection

Like most researchers I know who have been designing questionnaires for twenty tears, I have grown accustomed to asking questions using a certain style and approach, that is rooted in asking the respondent how they feel or think in respect of their own personal point of view about their own decision making. For example, "Q. How will you vote at the next general election. The emphasis is on the personal - how they will vote.

ICM, the UK polling company, use a method called the 'Wisdom Index". Instead of asking how the respondent will vote, it asks them to predict who will win the next general election.

We could take this approach further to other common scenarios in market research. For example, asking respondents which brand of mobile phone will sell the most as opposed to which brand they are more likely to buy. Or instead of asking how much they would pay for a product, ask the respondent to predict what price on a scale they think the product will be sold at. Some researchers have demonstrated that asking questions bases on prediction or on how they think other people will behave results in data which is more closely aligned with actual outcomes.

Context and Personalisation

Another technique is to ask respondents to imagine themselves in a particular context before asking the question. For example, "Q. Imagine you were in charge of TV schedules. Can you draw up a list of programmes you would like to show on your main channel". The question would be an open ended question.

Reported Behaviour

Many questions are based around asking what the respondent likes. For example, "Q. What are your favourite TV programmes"? An alternative approach is to ask about actual behaviour. For example, "Q. What did you watch on TV last night? Followed by, "Q. If there had been a film on at the same time, how likely would you have been to watch that instead?".

Gamification and New Approaches

Gamification in market research is very current, and there is a great deal of innovation in the field. It can take a number of forms, but at its heart, it is the attempt to build rules and context into questionnaires in a way we would recognise in a game.

> Its a very exciting time to experiment with questionnaire design, and in many ways the rules of questionnaire design are in a state of flux.

That's not to say that the ground rules of planning questionnaires and asking unambiguous questions are not relevant. They are, but at the same time, many trusted approaches and question styles are being reconsidered. Matrix questions are an obvious target.

At the moment, gamification is a shiny new thing for innovative researchers and is not widely accessible in affordable survey tools. That will change over time, and I predict that gamifying approaches and tools will become more mainstream.

Here are a few examples of how gamification is already being used.

Respondent as Judge

Instead of asking how well a broadband provider performs, we can encourage the respondent to be a judge and if so how they would judge the brand on a range of factors. In reality it is not very different from asking about performance, except that the respondent is being persuaded to play the game of being a judge on a panel. Another variation is "Q.

Imagine you owned a radio station. Which of these artists would you feature?"

Word Counts

Instead of asking how you would describe a brand, ask to describe the brand in exactly seven words.

Time Limits

This technique is similar to word counts insofar as it sets a rule. The question might have a 60 seconds or 2 minute time frame. I was fortunate enough to work with a BBC TV quiz programme for a few years called Pointless. We provided polling services for the show, where many of the questions were time based. The respondent could advance to the next question, but if they couldn't complete the question, at the end of the time period, the questionnaire automatically advanced to the next question.

Points Based Rewards

Nike sports have a number of sports products designed to encourage people to compete with themselves. Nike Fuel is a point based system which is rewarded to users of sports watches which calculate how many calories the user has burnt during measured exercise routines. Some questionnaires use a similar approach. For example, a question which asks the respondent to name as many ads they can remember. The respondent would get a point for each correct answer, and then be shown the result at the end of the question as an instant feedback.

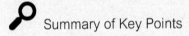

Summary of Key Points

Good questionnaire design comes with practice. The aim is not perfection, but to design surveys which have clear an unambiguous questions.

Be clear about your Survey Plan before starting to design the questionnaire.

Plan out the contents, topics and structure of the questionnaire before writing the detailed questions and designing the questionnaire.

Familiarise yourself with the types of questions available in a survey package and look at ready-made-templates available in survey tools before designing a questionnaire.

In general, it is usually easier to design a questionnaire in a word processor before scripting it in a survey tool. It's easier to make changes and review early drafts of a questionnaire before it is scripted in the survey tool.

Suggested Follow Up Exercise

Refer back to chapter 7 to review key considerations for planning a survey

Review a free Survey template to check the common types of question styles.

Refer back to chapter 8 to look at common question types used in Survey tools.

Experiment with different ways of asking questions including traditional and alternative methods.

Pick a survey topic. Then experiment with the process of planning the questionnaire, before designing the questionnaire in a word processor.

Programming Your Survey

The terms *programming*, *scripting* and *hosting* are often used interchangeably by online research professionals. Programming a survey is in essence taking a questionnaire typically written in a word processor and converting it into a working survey script on an online survey tool.

 Programming and scripting are terms used interchangeably: they refer to converting a written questionnaire into a working online survey.

Given the sheer range of survey tools, each with a different interface, question types and rules, it is impossible to demonstrate how to script (or programme) a survey for all survey tools in the market.

There are dozens of well known web based and enterprise survey tools, and possibly hundreds of lesser known tools and applications.

 Enterprise Survey Tool

An enterprise survey tool is designed to be used across large organisations. It may have multiple users accounts and will feature ways of sharing data or reports across the organisation.

But a web based survey tool like Surveygoo will share many similar concepts with other recognised web based tools used for building online survey scripts.

This chapter will demonstrate the process and relevant considerations for converting a questionnaire into a working script. To follow the example, and to practice scripting your own survey, it is recommended you sign up to a Freemium subscription of Surveygoo, if you have not already done so.

> We also recommend that you download the Surveygoo Guide, called Quick Guide: Surveygoo Walkthrough, which is available on the Quick Guides Tutorial Page.

Setting Up a New Questionnaire Script

To set up a new survey in Surveygoo, click on the New Survey tab or the Create Survey button in the dashboard.

You will then see the Define Survey page, where you will need to give the survey a title, select a survey category and to select the sample source (e.g. define how the survey will be distributed).

There are currently four sample sources which can be defined with Surveygoo:

- [x] Other
- [x] Own Sample
- [x] External Sample
- [x] Blend Sample

Other - share the survey URL later, either on a website, social media, email campaign (using an external client package such as outlook) or publish it offline, such as on a postcard or letter.

Own Sample - share the survey via your own email database, which is distributed via the Surveygoo Email Management System. This is an easy way to upload a database, then share the survey without having to use external email systems. Many survey tools will have their own email management system included in the software.

External Sample - Surveygoo is integrated with various online research panels, allowing the user to launch a survey with external consumers who are members of online panels. It is also possible to use external research panels but the External Sample tab connects directly with Surveygoo's Online Panel Access facility. The main advantage is the ease with which a panel survey can be run (e.g. the whole panel management process is integrated in the software).

Blend Sample - For surveys where online panel access and your own email database are to be used at the same time.

Questionnaire Example

For the purposes of the demonstration we shall be using a ready made questionnaire template called Customer Satisfaction - PR agency. We will also be assuming that this is a survey being conducted using a client database.

Cloning a Survey

To use one of the available questionnaire templates in the tool click on a relevant template located at the top of the Dashboard, and click on Create Copy.

In the How to Use area of the Resources section of the Surveygoo website there is a guide on Using templates.

There is also a Screencast demonstrating how to use templates.

It is also possible to re-use (clone) a previous survey you have launched in your account from the Archive area in the dashboard, which is a database all the previous surveys you have conducted.

Having clicked on the Create Copy link, the questionnaire template (in this case, Customer Satisfaction - PR Agency) will be selected ready to use again. The Define Survey page is loaded, pre populated with the survey details defined in the questionnaire template. Click the Next button to proceed to the Design Survey stage.

Designing the Survey

The Design Survey page contains all the defined questions, and features for programming the survey.

Navigating your Way Round the Design Survey Page

Each page of the questionnaire is displayed in order, and on each page individual questions created will appear. The actual questions appear on the lower section of the page. Consider each of these as a single page which are joined together in sequence. Click on the Add Page link to add pages; all current pages are listed beneath the Add Page title as a series of individual page links.

Under the pages links are three other key functions:

- ☑ Demographic Questions

- ☑ Qualifying Questions

- ☑ Question Routing

Demographic Questions

Demographic Questions is a facility to include in the questionnaire fields for collecting age, gender, country, region and other demographic criteria. It's not essential to include demographics at the front of the questionnaire (e.g. sometimes researchers include these at the end) but in many cases demographic questions are included at the beginning of a questionnaire, along with relevant screening criteria.

Qualifying Questions

The generic term Qualifying Question, is any question or set of questions used to target and screen for respondents, based on the answer they give to the qualifying question(s). You can ask as many qualifying questions as you like, typically within the first few questions of the survey. Surveygoo has a Qualifying Question function, which is featured at the top of the Survey Design page. It should be used when running a survey with Online Panel Access. It functions as with any screening question insofar as respondents will qualify or be disqualified to do the survey based on this question. The reason for using it with Online Panel Access is that it allows the user to only pay for sample which qualifies for the survey (assuming the response rate is more than 33%). Read more about Online Panel Access in chapter 12.

 The generic term Qualifying Question is any question or set of questions used to target and screen respondents, based on the answer they give.

Question Routing

Question routing is common in most survey tools, including lower end tools. In some surveys it is necessary to route respondents through to certain questions based on the answers they have given to previous questions. The advantage of using page routing (or conditional routing as it is sometimes called) is that it make the respondent experience more relevant by making sure only relevant questions are being asked. For example, there is little point in asking questions which cannot be answered by the respondent because they do not fit the criteria. Question routing is a useful technique, but it is important that the logical flow of a questionnaire is carefully established, including routing, when the questionnaire is being designed.

The advantage of question routing is that it improves the respondent experience by making the questionnaire more relevant to them.

Adding Questions

All available question types are shown at the top right of the Design Survey page. Click on the icon of the question type to add a question. Each question is set up using a simple wizard. There are differences between which fields are required in the question set up, depending on the question type, but most question styles require a) a question; and b) question answers (also known as answer codes). Other common considerations include whether the question answers are single choice or multiple choice, whether to include images or video, use of none of the above and don't know options as standard, whether the question should be mandatory (so that all respondents are forced to answer the question) and for the answers to be randomized (e.g. so that the order of the answer codes appear in a randomized order). See chapter 8 (Question Types) and chapter 9 (Designing Questionnaires) for more information on key question types and considerations of how to use them.

Applying Theme Designs

One way to improve the look and feel of a questionnaire is to use different theme designs. Surveygoo has a number of different theme designs which consist of backgrounds, frames and a progress bar. You can select an overall theme design and accept the settings, or also modify the theme as necessary. The selected theme is displayed at the bottom of the Design Survey page. When ready, click the Next button to proceed to launch stage.

 Survey themes are an easy way to make a survey look and feel more interesting to respondents.

There is also a Screencast demonstrating how to use theme designs.

Preview Survey

At the Launch Survey stage, it is still possible to go back a stage and make last minute amendments to the questionnaire. To review the questionnaire, click on the Preview Survey button. A test version of the survey is then displayed so that it can be evaluated from the perspective of a survey respondent. The preview survey is a full test, allowing you to click through the survey and making selections to the questions. This is essential for checking that page routing is working and that the questionnaire appears as was intended. Now is the time to double check question wording, answer options, spelling, and programming requirements like randomization and mandatory questions. When you are satisfied, click on the Launch Survey button.

 Always preview a survey before launching it to avoid sending a survey with basic mistakes.

In this example, the survey would be distributed with a database of customers using the Email Management System. See chapter 12 for more information.

Other Key Programming Requirements: Quotas and Piping

Quota controls and piping are widely used when scripting an online survey. They are not essential for every survey, but they are important concepts to be considered.

Survey Quota Controls

Quota controls (or quota management as it is sometimes called) in online surveys allow the survey programmer to control the number of respondents who complete the survey by specified demographics and other criteria.

Key Programming Functions

☑ Survey Quota Controls

☑ Question Piping

☑ Answer Piping

Control Gender to be Nationally Representative

A common example of quota controls in online surveys is limiting the number of interviews to be completed by gender. In a nationally representative survey of the UK, we would expect to receive approximately 48% Males and 52% Female (this is the proportion of each gender in the national population). So in a survey of 100 people, if the sample fell out naturally we would expect to get 48 men and 52 women in the sample of 100 completes.

Often panel samples are adjusted automatically to get the correct level of distribution. Online Panel Access ensures that the correct distribution of samples are invited to a survey, assuming a sample of 200 or more but the actual completes may not be exactly representative of the population. To ensure we definitely receive the exact number of completes by gender, we should set quota controls.

Control Gender Disproportionately

In other cases, we may want to adjust gender quota controls to be disproportionately higher for a particular gender. For example, a producer of salad leaves may want to survey potential customers. It knows that a higher proportion of women make the purchasing decision in weekly supermarket shopping and it is particularly interested in the views of Waitrose shoppers, because they are more likely to pay for premium salad products. The quota for women could be set to 70% for example, and we could also control the number of Waitrose shoppers at say 20% (compared with its overall market share of perhaps 5%) by setting a quota from a question on the respondent's preferred supermarket for the weekly shop. We could also target Waitrose shoppers in a sample selection from the online research panel we are using.

 Quota Management

The active management of setting quotas and monitoring the progress of the status of achieved, and achievable quotas in a survey.

Independent Quotas

Many online surveys of nationally representative populations use Independent Quota Controls. Each quota is controlled independently e.g. setting a control of 100 completes in 18-34 age bracket ensures a maximum of 100 completes in this age group. However, it does not ensure that the split between gender within the age group is correct. In all likelihood the gender split within the age group will be close to the national distribution (assuming that the panel provider has responsive and representative panel membership), but it is not likely to be exact. If we have a series of independent quotas on age, gender and region, each quota individually can be set to be representative of the quota criteria individually.

The main advantages of independent quotas is that they are simple to set up, and more importantly, quicker, cheaper and faster to fill when respondents answer the survey. The disadvantage is that it is likely that the sample will not be representative of criteria within the quotas (e.g. representative of age and region within gender).

Interlocking Quotas

The key difference with an interlocking quota is that it enables full control over the sample by more than one quota control simultaneously. For example, age and gender together. That means controlling the sample of 25-49 year olds, for example, by gender as well as age so that the proportion of men and women within this age demographic reflect the true proportion of men and women by age group in the population.

The main advantage of interlocking quotas is that it is the only way to guarantee sample properly reflects the real population distribution. But there are important disadvantages, which are the opposite of those for Independent Quotas. They take longer to calculate and to program (all quotas require manual set up) and more significantly, will increase the fieldwork times and possibly the cost to fulfill the required sample responses.

What type of Quota Control is Best?

Technically, Interlocking Quotas deliver the most representative samples. But from a practical sense, Independent Quotas are easier to use and more cost effective. First, it takes less time to calculate and set up Independent Quotas. Second, the time to fill Independent Quotas is much shorter than Interlocking Quotas. Although panel sample in developed digital economies, like the UK, are large and representative, there are still limitations. Setting Independent Quotas for age, gender and region, will always be easier to fill than Interlocking Quotas, especially when you consider some UK regions and countries have much smaller panels (e.g. Wales, Northern Ireland and Scotland). Our recommendation is that in many instances, Independent Quotas are simpler and fit for purpose for many, if not most surveys.

Programming Independent Sample Quotas

Surveygoo includes functionality for Independent Sample Quotas. See the How to Guide, Using Independent Sample Quotas, in the How to area of the Resources section of the Surveygoo website.

Question Piping

Question piping is a common feature in online surveys. The idea is to pass on answers from a previous question into the wording of a subsequent question or questions. For example, a question may ask what type of bank account the respondent has. If the respondent selects a particular bank account (e.g. Savings account), a second question which asks if they have access to online banking for that account would appear with the relevant bank type directly within the question. The question would read, "Do you have access to your Savings Account through online banking?"

To see an example of Question Piping and learn how to set up Question Piping in Surveygoo, see the How to section of the Resources area of the website, and look for the article, Using Question Piping.

Answer Piping

Answer Piping is similar to Question Piping insofar as it is a way to pass on answers through to subsequent questions. While Question Piping pipes into question titles, Answer Piping pipes through to the answer codes of questions. The How to Guide, Using Answer Piping provides a working example of Answer Piping in a live questionnaire, and how to set up questions with answer piping in Surveygoo.

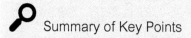 Summary of Key Points

Programming and scripting are terms used interchangeably: they refer to converting a written questionnaire into a working online survey.

The generic term Qualifying Question is any question or set of questions used to target and screen respondents, based on the answer they give.

The advantage of question routing is that it improves the respondent experience by making the questionnaire more relevant to them.

Survey themes are an easy way to make a survey look and feel more interesting to respondents.

Always preview a survey before launching it to avoid sending a survey with basic mistakes.

Suggested Follow Up Exercises

Refer back to chapter 8 to review key question types and chapter 9 for the key considerations when designing questionnaires.

Watch the Screencast: Surveygoo Dashboard.

Refer to Quick Guide: Surveygoo Walkthrough.

Clone the Question Template, Customer Satisfaction - PR Agency.

Review each question type created in the questionnaire template within the edit question function.

Section 5
Sharing and
Distributing Surveys

11: Final Checks

12: Sharing an Email Survey

13: Using Online Panels

This section covers the main options for sharing online surveys with survey participants.

In chapter 11 we cover the last minute checks and tests before launching a survey.

Chapter 12 provides an overview of common methods to share a survey by email as well as key issues around anti spam legislation and good practice for designing email invitations .

Chapter 13 takes a closer look at how to use online survey panels and key issues to be aware of before selecting an online panel.

Final Checks: Preview, Tests and Pilots

"Quality is not an act, it is a habit"

Aristotle

You can never spend enough time checking a survey before launching it. In chapter 9 we looked at the 5 stages of questionnaire design. The 5th stage was to "review, test and pilot the questionnaire".

There are two distinct parts of the questionnaire to check. Firstly, the draft questionnaire before the questionnaire is programmed (or scripted) in the survey tool. Secondly, the survey script.

In one sense, potential critical errors of the questionnaire should have been identified and removed by now. If you have followed the 4 previous steps recommended in chapter 9 (e.g. have a survey plan; plan the questionnaire; review and select questions; write the questionnaire) you will have gone a long way to ensure that you have planned and implemented the questionnaire design in a well planned way. Stage 5 (reviewing, testing and piloting) a survey is very important, so take as much time as you can on this stage.

Assuming the questionnaire was checked before it was programmed, there is a last round of checks to do for the survey script once it has been programmed in the survey tool. There are several ways this can be done.

Final Checks

- ☑ Preview survey script
- ☑ Share test link with colleagues
- ☑ Run a test survey
- ☑ Pilot a live survey

Preview Survey Script

Most survey tools should allow the programmer to review the survey script before it is launched. In Surveygoo, the user has the choice of going to the Launch Page to check the survey in Preview mode. By clicking on the Preview mode (or reviewing the survey test link), it is possible to go through the survey and fully test it before moving to the final step and launching a live survey. This provides the opportunity to check for any errors in the questionnaire design, but more likely, at this stage, it can reveal last minute changes to the look, feel and pagination of the survey.

Share Test Link with Colleagues

In many cases it is possible to self review the questionnaire in preview mode. However, if there is sufficient time and you have the option to share a scripted survey with a colleague, it is recommended that you do. In some cases, a team working on a project may want to be involved, and in other cases, you may have an individual in mind who are good at proof reading.

Surveygoo publishes the test link when using Other as the sample source, but you can also share the Preview link by copying and pasting the url when looking at the survey in Preview mode.

Run a Test Survey

Running a test survey is an extension of checking a test link. The idea is to distribute the survey to a handful of individuals who will complete the survey, as a means of checking the survey effectively as a live survey. Apart from checking the survey script, it's also an opportunity to check the data in terms of the data being collected (e.g. the format of the data collected for the questions are as intended). As with sharing the test link, the Test Survey participants are likely to be internal (project team members and colleagues) as opposed to actual respondents. A Test Survey is an effective extension of a thorough Preview test, but in many cases there isn't the time to include it. It's certainly worthwhile if you have the time or are less experienced at scripting and checking your own work.

Pilot a Live Survey

The last type of survey review is called a Pilot Survey. The difference between a pilot and a Test Survey is that it is a more thorough exercise, typically involved more time to check the results including a potential pause in the survey, and crucially, involves using a live sample of respondents rather than the internal project team. It provides the opportunity not only to check the survey script and the type of data generated, but potentially to make some judgements about the survey design (e.g. the audience, the sample incidence rate, etc) which can feed into designing a main, or second phase of a larger survey.

Professional market researchers may pilot surveys, depending on the scale, budget and timing of the project. I can recall a time when running Pilots or even Soft Pilots (e.g. a light touch pilot where the survey was reviewed but not necessarily paused) was used frequently. But in my experience, Piloting has become less common, perhaps in response to cost, but more probably, in response to the need to conduct surveys more quickly and with ever shortening deadlines. But a Pilot is certainly worth considering if the time is available, or there is significant uncertainty in the way a survey should be designed. Equally, it could be that it makes sense to conduct a small scale survey to test key assumptions about a product or service before moving on to a larger scale exercise.

Sharing an Email Survey

For many people, an online survey is synonymous with an email survey. A database of email addresses is used to send survey invitations; the person receiving such an email clicks on a link which takes them to a website where they can view and complete the survey. Surveys conducted using market research panels (which we introduced in chapter 3) are often managed in a similar way. Online and digital surveys continue to evolve with the huge growth of smart phones and tablet devices. Surveys can be conducted specifically for mobile phone users with panel samples via mobile phones. But at this time, many, if not most online surveys, are still conducted using an email invitation.

In the next chapter we will take a hands on view of how market research panels can be used via a survey tool. In this chapter we will look at the email driven survey using a database of contacts.

The Simplicity of Email Surveys

The email based survey is perfect for organisations looking to conduct a DIY survey. Theoretically at least, conducting your own survey with your customers or a database of email addresses is tantalising simple. Surely it's just a case of adding some questions, writing an email, pressing a button and then waiting for your survey to be completed. Easy as 1,2,3. Right?

Wrong!

> Yes, in principle conducting a survey with a software tool like Surveygoo is very manageable, dare I say easy. But only if we take a careful approach to planning, designing and implementing the survey.

We have seen some key aspects of planning a survey, designing a questionnaire and programming it in a survey tool. However, there are a number of pitfalls to navigate when we are ready to launch an email survey that uses email databases. One key aspect is the area of spam policy and spam filters which combine a policy of ethical best practice with the technical practicalities of email communications. Another key aspect is writing survey invitations which are not only compliant with market research practice, but at the same time attract and persuade respondents to complete surveys.

 Email survey invitations need to be inviting to prompt action, but they also need to comply with best practice to avoid being seen as spam.

What is spam?

The chance is you have heard of it, have experienced it and probably take a strong dislike to it! Most of us don't like spam, so we should be careful not to create spam ourselves. Spam is of course any email communication received by people who have no relationship with or knowledge of the sender. A database which has been collated without the knowledge or consent of the person whose details are being used is quite simply spam.

Databases which have been built without the knowledge and consent of the receiver the email is spam.

Spam Surveys Bomb!

Marketeers who use databases which have not been built on a permission or opt-in basis will get chronically poor response rates. It's amazing how there are still so many less than honourable companies selling databases of consumers or businesses which have been built with questionable practices. Even those built using some means of permission mechanism are often not great. Just as cold calling is seen as poor practice, and less and less effective, so are many databases.

Surveys sent to databases of individuals where there is no relationship between the sender and recipient will also attract very poor response rates. There is no such thing as a cheap database, and no short cuts to compiling a database which is legally compliant but is also effective. So there are very practical reasons for not sending survey invitations to anonymous databases. We cover good and bad examples of database sources below.

Spam Legislation in the UK

The other reason why we need to be very aware of spam when sending an email survey is that we want to ensure our survey complies with not only good business practice, but also the law of the land! The Privacy and Electronic Communications Regulations 2003 Act covers the sending of email marketing (including for surveys) which falls under the remit of the Information Commissioner's Office (ICO). It defines the need for UK organisations to ensure that it does not send emails to individuals who have not opted in to be sent email communication. The ICO website (www.ico.org.uk) provides a lot of useful information on the requirements of organisations to comply with this legislation and the Data Protection Act.

Anti Spam Policies of Survey Tool Companies

Since the issue of spam is a legal issue as well as one of ethical and good business practice, it is not surprising that survey tools carry clear terms and conditions for its users to comply with anti spam legislation.

 Survey tools carry clear terms of use requirements around anti spam legislation which must be complied with.

Generally these terms and conditions mirror the requirements of the Anti Spam legislation (e.g. CAN-

SPAM Act of 2003 in US and The Privacy and Electronic Communications Regulations 2003 Act in the UK). If a user breaches these terms and conditions, they will have crossed a red line and can suffer the consequences, ultimately being prevented from using the survey software. I had a colleague who was banned from using the Mail Chimp email client in the US because the spam filters (see below) identified an unacceptable level of spam. The database used to conduct the survey had been provided by the client; it didn't matter that it was ultimately the client's database team which had provided databases which did not comply.

Its now very easy to report spam, In fact it is positively encouraged by ISPs. The fact is the threshold is actually quite low for complaints about spam to have an impact on mail delivery services. Direct Mail for Apple, for example, says complaint rates of just over 0.01% (just 5 complaints in 50,000 recipients) can result in a degrading of services or even a blacklisting. Apart from the anti spam legislation, consumers may be less willing to put up with spam. Their pain threshold is perhaps lower than it used to be, and many will simply complain rather than click on the unsubscribe link.

So the message is clear - be very careful when sending email invitations to people. Keep an exceptionally clean and well maintained database, seek permission to send emails, and do not use cheap, purchased databases. Arguably, samples provided by panel companies is one of the best ways to ensure that you are using opt in, quality assured sample. These sample (databases) have been built 100% on an opt in basis.

Spam Traps: Avoiding Spam Filters

Most people will have some form of spam filter on their PC, Mac or digital device. Different programs function differently to identify unsolicited and unwanted emails, and prevent emails getting into the inbox. The concern if you are running an email survey is that you don't want your survey invite going straight to the spam or junk folder, raising the prospect that the potential respondents never see your survey invite. You may have a database which was built in an opt in basis and conforms to every good practice for building and maintaining a list.

 "Opt In" Database

A database built where the person is invited to join the database, rather than being automatically added to a database and given the option to "opt out". Opting in is often viewed as better practice.

None of that matters if the email invitation triggers a spam filter; the survey will be invisible to all intents and purposes.

There is no guarantee that your survey invitation will not get caught in a spam filter, no matter how hard you try to conform to good practice.

But at the very least ensure:

- ☑ Send emails to a database of individuals who have opted in to a list, and have an expectation of receiving emails

- ☑ State how and why the person is being sent the survey invite

- ☑ Make it clear that the exercise is a genuine market research exercise

- ☑ Always include an option to opt out of the database

To enhance response rates, consider offering an incentive (such as a prize draw) or donation to charity. If it is a business survey you could offer a free report and summary of the survey results.

Many of the email client software include automatic checks to ensure the email conforms to good practice of email design.

Low risk of being marked as spam

"Surveygoo users nl Dec2013" scored 0 on SpamAssassin

Issues

(none)

Reminders

● Your email should include clear unsubscribe instructions

● Your email should include your physical address and phone number (i.e. non-Internet contact information)

● Your email should explain why the recipient was added to your mailing list

How to Send the Survey Invite

Surveygoo includes an inbuilt email sender function. Users can upload a database, and create an email invitation directly within the survey tool. This has the advantage of using a simple means to create a survey invite and sending it via the email system. It saves time and means you do not have to pay for third party applications.

 The concern for running an email survey is that the invites get trapped in spam filters, raising the prospect that the respondent doesn't see the survey invitation.

However, there are many alternative email clients (applications) you can consider. There are too many to cover here, but leading examples include dotmailer.co.uk (which is a web based email application) and for Apple users, Direct Mail (directmailmac.com) which is accessed from the desktop.

 Email Client

An application to send, read or manage emails. e.g. Outlook, Mac Mail, or email campaign tools such as dotmailer.co.uk.

The main advantage of using third party email clients is the often detailed reporting features (to track the response rates and effectiveness of the campaigns) and the ability to design great looking emails.

What to Say in an Invitation Email

If you are using an online research panel to reach your sample, you don't need to worry about email invitation scripts because the panel company will handle it. (See chapter 12 on Using Online Panels). But if you are sending an email invitation to a customer base or an email database, you will need to write a compelling message. The email invitation is a very important step (in many ways as important as designing the questionnaire) because persuading people to take the time to complete a survey is not as easy as it sounds. The message you write needs to trigger an action: for someone to complete your survey. But email response rates are typically very low and can also vary enormously depending on the source of the sample and the purpose of the survey. It could be as low as 0.5% or a customer survey with an engaged customer base could attract a response rate of 5 or 15%.

We touched on earlier the need to state the purpose of the survey, and to indicate where the database has been sourced from.

But in addition you should consider:

▶ Mentioning the MRS Code of Conduct

▶ Offering an incentive (financial or other kind of reward)

▶ Stating how the survey data will be used

▶ Indicate specific dates to complete the survey

MRS Code of Conduct

The Market Research Society is the custodian of good market research practice in the UK. If you or a consultant involved in the project is a member of the MRS, they should state that they are or that the survey is being conducted in line with the Code of Practice of the Market Research Society, and that any data provided by the respondent will not be directly attributed to individuals. e.g. individual comments from the survey and responses given will not be made public as to who has said them. This is key for most surveys but particularly for employee surveys where individuals must feel confident that any negative responses they may provided in a survey won't come back to haunt them!

Example Invitation Letters

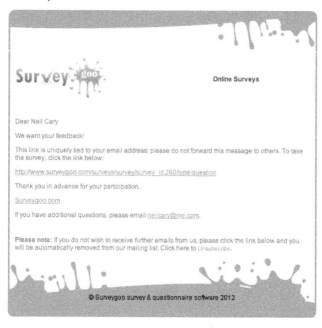

Survey goo   **Online Surveys**

Dear Neil Cary

We want your feedback!

This link is uniquely tied to your email address; please do not forward this message to others. To take the survey, click the link below:

http://www.surveygoo.com/surveys/survey/survey_id:260/type:question

Thank you in advance for your participation.

Surveygoo.com

If you have additional questions, please email neilcary@me.com.

Please note: If you do not wish to receive further emails from us, please click the link below and you will be automatically removed from our mailing list: Click here to Unsubscribe.

© Surveygoo survey & questionnaire software 2012

Survey goo   **Customer Feedback**

Dear Neil Cary

We invite you to participate in a short online survey. Your feedback is important to us and we appreciate your time. This survey will take just a few minutes to complete, and we will only use your feedback to improve our services.

This link is uniquely tied to your email address; please do not forward this message to others. To take the survey, click the link below:

http://www.surveygoo.com/surveys/survey/survey_id:262/type:question

Thank you in advance for your participation.

Rainbow Au Pairs

If you have additional questions, please email neil@rainbowaupairs.co.uk.

Please note: If you do not wish to receive further emails from us, please click the link below and you will be automatically removed from our mailing list: Click here to Unsubscribe.

© Surveygoo survey & questionnaire software 2012

Member Survey

Dear Neil Cary

CSTN would like to invite you to take part in a short online survey about your experience of **CSTN Events.**

By taking part in this survey, you will be providing vital feedback which will be used to improve our events in the future.

The survey is being conducted in line with the Market Research Society Code of Conduct. **Your individual responses will remain anonymous and only be used for the purposes of improving our events and services to members.**

The survey takes approximately 5 minutes. Please be as honest and full with your responses as possible. With your feedback we can continue to change and improve our service to our members.

This link is uniquely tied to your email address: please do not forward this message to others. To take the survey, click the link below:

http://www.surveygoo.com/surveys/survey/survey_id:284

Thank you in advance for your participation.

Surveygoo.com

If you have additional questions, please email neilcary@me.com.

Please note: If you do not wish to receive further emails from us, please click the link below and you will be automatically removed from our mailing list: Click here to Unsubscribe.

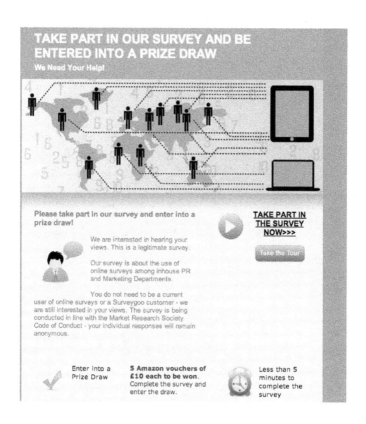

TAKE PART IN OUR SURVEY AND BE ENTERED INTO A PRIZE DRAW

We Need Your Help!

Please take part in our survey and enter into a prize draw!

TAKE PART IN THE SURVEY NOW>>>

Take the Tour

We are interested in hearing your views. This is a legitimate survey.

Our survey is about the use of online surveys among inhouse PR and Marketing Departments.

You do not need to be a current user of online surveys or a Surveygoo customer - we are still interested in your views. The survey is being conducted in line with the Market Research Society Code of Conduct - your individual responses will remain anonymous.

Enter into a Prize Draw

5 Amazon vouchers of £10 each to be won. Complete the survey and enter the draw.

Less than 5 minutes to complete the survey

Offering Incentives

Incentives can vary from being entered into a prize draw, a financial reward or a charity donation. If your company can offer discounts or give away free products you need to check that it doesn't contradict rules of best practice. For example, the MRS recommends linking surveys to rewards if the reward is a company's own product. For business to business surveys, providing a copy of the survey results can be incentive enough to participate in a survey, if the data is relevant to the audience.

Purpose of the Survey

If people are giving up their time to complete a survey the least we can do is tell them what the survey is for, why they should take the survey, and what they are getting out of the exercise. It's not necessary to provide sensitive commercial information, but if a customer survey or product test will have a direct input into improving customer experience or will result in new product offerings, why not tell them!

Practical Fieldwork details

It is often a good idea to indicate how long the survey will be running for. If no fieldwork dates are provided, the respondent may not respond to the survey quickly. Equally, choose the time and day carefully to send a survey invite. Weekends are probably not a good idea for some consumers (e.g. busy mums) or for business audiences on a monday morning.

There is no exact formula for choosing the best time and day for a survey invite but try to think when the audience is more likely to be receptive.

You can also send email reminders but make sure you don't send emails to people who have already completed the survey or have indicated they want to be unsubscribed from the database. The majority of survey responses are made between 3 and 7 days from the time of the survey invite, so it is not worth sending reminder emails before 3 or 4 days from the start date.

 Offering an incentive is a good way of encouraging a response to a survey. It can include a prize draw but business surveys can offer different incentives, such as a free copy of the survey results.

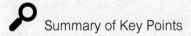 Summary of Key Points

Email survey invitations need to be inviting to prompt action, but they also need to comply with best practice to avoid being seen as spam.

Databases which have been built without the knowledge and consent of the receiver the email is spam.

Survey tools carry clear terms of use requirements around anti spam legislation which must be complied with.

The concern for running an email survey is that the invites get trapped in spam filters, raising the prospect that the respondent doesn't see the survey invitation.

Offering an incentive is a good way of encouraging a response to a survey. It can include a prize draw but business surveys can offer different incentives, such as a free copy of the survey results.

Suggested Follow Up Exercises

Review current spam legislation and best practice guidelines published on the ICO website ico.org.uk

Look at MRS Guidelines on Incentives and Standards published on the MRS website:

www.mrs.org.uk/standards/faqs

Refer to How to Guide 'Sending Email Invitations' in the Surveygoo Resources area.

Using Online Panels

Online Panels have become a very popular choice for conducting online surveys. It's not hard to see why: they are affordable, flexible and highly accessible. At the same time they offer excellent opportunities for targeting specific audiences, based on detailed profiling information.

We covered the basics of online panels in chapter 3, Overview of Online Panels). If you skipped this chapter before, and would like to have a summary of online panels, now would be a good time to go back to chapter 3.

This chapter is looking at the practical issues of using online panels. Specifically, we will look at running a so called feasibility (to see if there are sufficient panellists available) and the costs of using panels.

But the main focus of the chapter is effectively a How to Guide, to run a survey using an online panel. For the purposes of this exercise, we will be using Surveygoo, and specifically, our Online Panel Access tool.

Finally, we will look at the end to end process of using online panels.

Checking Feasibility and Costs of Panels

Accessing Panels

There are literally thousands of panels and panel companies to choose from of different sizes and capabilities around the world. But there are only handful of global providers. There is so much choice it can take a lot of time finding and evaluating providers. Surveygoo maintains its own panels, called Opini in 9 countries. But Surveygoo survey tool also features an API which allows users of the survey tool to connect with hundreds of research panels in more than 50 countries. This, in our view, is one of the easiest ways to run an online survey with research panels without worrying about surveys links, and other technical aspects of panel administration.

Checking Panel Feasibility

The fastest way to check panel feasibility for general online panels directly accessible in the Surveygoo survey tool is to use the Feasibility and Price Calculator function, which is hosted on the Surveygoo website.

To use the calculator follow these steps:

Go to the survey tool plans page...

www.Surveygoo.com/packages

Scroll to the bottom of the page and look for the box named Online Panel Access.

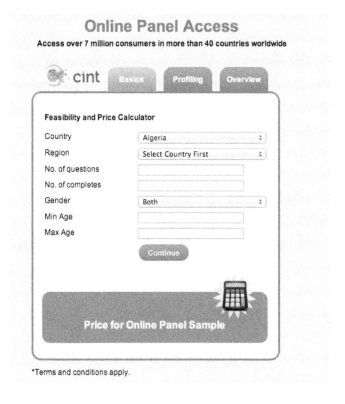

Next, fill out the basic fields shown under the Basics tab:

▶ County

▶ Region

▶ No. of questions

▶ No. of survey completes required (responses)

▶ Gender

▶ Age

The calculator also shows three options under profiling:

▶ Education Level

▶ Occupation Status

▶ Household income

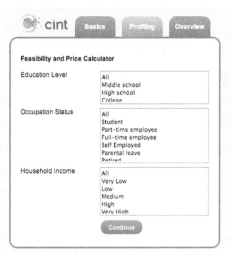

*Terms and conditions apply.

Once these have been selected, continue to the Overview page, which will confirm the selections, feasibility and costs of using the panels.

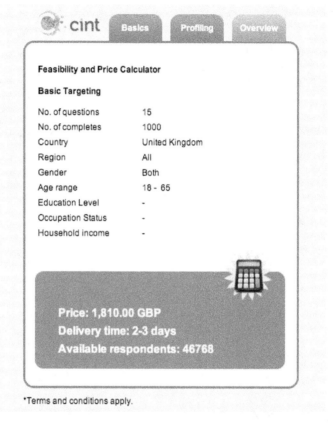

Feasibility and Price Calculator

Basic Targeting

No. of questions	15
No. of completes	1000
Country	United Kingdom
Region	All
Gender	Both
Age range	18 - 65
Education Level	-
Occupation Status	-
Household income	-

Price: 1,810.00 GBP
Delivery time: 2-3 days
Available respondents: 46768

*Terms and conditions apply.

The calculator is designed to provide a basic overview of panel feasibility and costs. Surveygoo users can run additional feasibility checks when they are conducting a survey within the tool.

Additional targeting options include:

- Marital status

- Household size

- Number of children

- Ages of children

- Personal income

- Company size

- Profession

- Field of expertise

- Car access

- Overseas travellers

Checking Panel Feasibility: Advanced Profiling

Many panel companies can also run a feasibility of reaching panel members by hundreds of different criteria. Chapter 3 includes examples of profiling criteria used by Opini to target panel members. These criteria can be used to estimate feasibility and costs for conducting a survey.

How to Access Panels in Surveygoo: Online Panel Access

Online Panel Access is a simple but powerful feature of Surveygoo survey tool. In simple terms Surveygoo has an API (called Cint Link) which seamlessly connects with a DIY panel selection tool. It enables the user to select, buy and run a survey directly within Surveygoo with research panels provided by the well known panel and technology company, Cint. There are no complex urls or codes to programme. The user just needs to select the panel sample source and follow the instructions to run the survey.

The broad process is as follows:

Step 1: Define the survey and select panel sample

Step 2: Design the survey questions

Step 3: Enter targeting requirements for the panel sample

Step 4: Launch and pay for the panel sample

Step 5: Wait for the results and review the data

It's really that simple. For a walkthrough of the detailed steps you need to go through, please review the How to Guide on the Surveygoo website, 'Online Panel Access'.

How to Access Panels in Surveygoo: Cint Access

The second DIY method for reaching panel sample in Surveygoo is called Cint Access. Cint Access provides superior targeting capabilities meaning that it is possible to reach highly profiled online panel samples across hundreds of data points, such as household data, consumer technology, cars, finance, shopping, travel and many more.

To use Cint Access, you will need to have an authorised account with Cint. Unlike the Online Panel Access solution, you will need to become familiar with the Cint system. While the process isn't automatic, Surveygoo has been designed to be compatible with Cint Access. You will need an appropriate subscription to allow you to amend the 'redirects' of the survey tool. For a full explanation of the process, please review the How to Guide, Survey Redirects and Access Panels.

It is by no means impossible for the less experienced user to work with Cint Access and the Surveygoo survey tool. However, it is recommended that if you are looking at the DIY route, you start with Online Panel Access. It offers the benefits of reaching quality assured online panels and is easy to use.

Of course, the alternative for using Cint Access is asking the Managed Service team at Surveygoo to design and conduct the survey on your behalf, but since the entire book is dedicated to the idea of the reader conducting their own surveys, I won't dwell on this option!

Suggested Follow Up Exercises

1. Look at How to Guide, Panel Sample Feasibility and Price.

2. Look at How to Guide, Online Panel Access.

3. Look at How to Guide, Survey Redirects and Access Panels.

4. There is also a Screencast demonstrating how to set up a demonstration survey using Online Panel Access which you can find on YouTube using this link: goo.gl/d6xz2U

Section 6
Analysis and Reporting

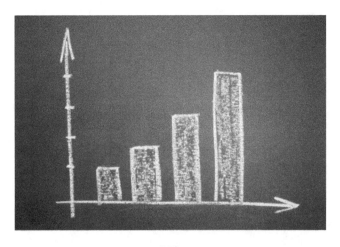

14: Reading Data

15: Data Quality

16: Common Words

This section provides an introduction to the key tools for analysing quantitative data collected in online surveys.

We start, in chapter 14, with the basic tools for reading data - top-line data and data tables, raw data and cross tabulations.

In chapter 15, we revisit the all important issue of data quality, with a closer look of how to address potential data quality issues with online panels.

Lastly, chapter 16 is called Common Words and Phrases used in Research. It is essentially a Glossary of research terms.

Reading Data

"If we knew what it was we were doing, it would not be called research"

Albert Einstein

You have designed a robust, engaging survey, and you have successfully collected your data. Now it's time to analyse the data. Depending on what you are looking to do with the analysis, the good news is that you do not need to be an expert statistician to get something out of the data. If you are familiar with analysing data, that's great. But if you are no expert in stats, it doesn't mean you have reached the end of the DIY survey journey.

Automation of Data Analysis

One of the benefits of using web based survey tools which has been designed for the would be DIY researcher is that there is a lot of data which is automatically generated within the tool, which can be easily accessed.

It then takes time, experience and some ability to develop your analytical skills. But it is by no means unrealistic to gain an insight into your market or customers from a survey tool which includes some key analytical tools.

In this chapter we will take a look at the core outputs of quantitative data analysis: the results dashboard, the PDF Top-line Report, Standard Data Tables and Cross Tabulations. In chapter 15, we will look at routes to more advanced analysis tools.

Data outputs automatically generated by Surveygoo are in common with many survey tools, and they include:

- ☑ Real Time Results Dashboard

- ☑ PDF (Top-line Report)

- ☑ Standard Data Tables

- ☑ Raw Data (Survey Responses Data)

- ☑ Cross Tabulations

- ☑ SPSS Data

Results Dashboard

The Results Dashboard is a very useful tool for keeping an eye on your survey results. Firstly, it provides real time results of a current survey in progress. For many people, once a survey is live, there is a compelling drive to keep tabs on how the survey results are progressing. Apart from satisfying curiosity, an early view of the survey results may be demanded by clients or relevant stakeholders, and arguably emerging yourself in the data as early as possible is good practice.

In Surveygoo, the Survey Reports Dashboard presents the responses to each question as a series of mini data tables. Unlike Standard Data Tables, the Results Dashboard shows the top-line of the data (e.g. the total results of all survey participants) rather than groups/breaks of data. If this idea is unfamiliar to you, we will cover this under Standard Data Tables.

Within the Results Dashboard view, you can toggle between Data Table, Bar and Pie Chart, as well as export charts (as PDF or JPEG images), and print individual question analysis. This is ideal at an early stage of the analysis, or when looking to show the story so far part way through the survey programme, in respect of a small number of key questions.

PDF Report

The PDF Report view is very similar to the Results Dashboard. It presents an overview of the results of each question. The data is displayed as individual data tables as opposed to charts. But, unlike the Results Dashboard, the results of all the questions are exported in a single report, which saves time to generate, and is an excellent way of starting the process of digesting the top-line results of the survey. For very simple surveys, quick polls, etc, it may be sufficient in itself for a limited analysis.

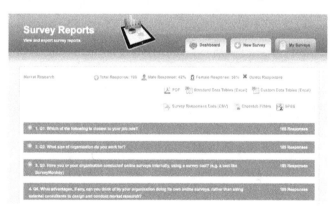

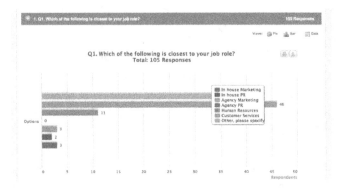

Views: Pie | Bar | Data

Options	Number of Respondents	Percentage
In house Marketing	3	3 %
In house PR	2	2 %
Agency Marketing	3	3 %
Agency PR	0	0 %
Human Resources	11	10 %
Customer Services	46	44 %
Other	40	38 %

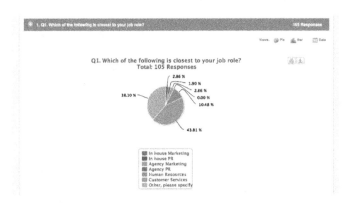

254 Reading Data

The Building Blocks of Data Analysis: Standard Data Tables

The core of any data analysis exercise is reviewing what are often called Data Tables.

Most quantitative survey data is presented as a computer or data tabulation, sometimes referred to as 'Data Tabs". Different software packages present data in slightly different ways; data analysis software tools provide extra options for formatting data and presenting statistical tests.

Standard Data Tables

Surveygoo provides a basic, but very easy to read format for data tables.

The Standard Data Tables downloaded from Surveygoo should be opened in Excel or another compatible software program as a spreadsheet.

The tables consist of:

▶ Columns – which show the breaks in the data, such as age or region

▶ Rows – which show question titles, and answer codes for each question

Reading Total Data

The question title is shown in bold blue, and includes a question no. reference. In line 11, in the above example, we see "1" which refers to the question number as stored in the Survegoo data file, followed by the question number reference and question text, used in the survey.

Directly underneath the question title is the Total, also known as the "base". This is the total number of people who answered the question. The Total is shown in Column E, row 13.

Underneath the total (rows 14 to 20), are the answer codes for the question. As with the Total, the number of cases who have an answer to each question code (answer) is shown in column E. For example, 3 people provided the answer "In house Marketing".

Since this was a single code question (each respondent provided one answer from the question options) the answer codes add to the base number for all the sample, which is 105.

The usual way to report data is to express the answers as a percentage. In column F, the % score have been calculated for each answer code of each question. So for Q1, the percentage result for the question answer "In house Marketing" was "2.86%".

Reading Column (Breaks)

The Standard Data Breaks in Surveygoo include Age, Gender, and Region. For example, Column K , row 13, shows 17 people answered the survey from London. We read the answers to question 1 for London survey participants, the same way as the Total column.

We can now compare the answers between the Total sample, and just London survey participants. So, we can see that for the answer "In House Marketing", whereas 3 out of 105 people, or 2.86% of the total sample gave this answer, among London it was 5.88% (1 out of 17). In this example, it would not be wise to assume that the results are statistically reliable (we would need at least 30 responses for London to start making comparisons with other groups). But this example demonstrates the way column data (or standard breaks) are read in data tables.

The principle is the same for reading additional column breaks (created in the Surveygoo Custom Data Tables feature) and similar for Cross Tabulations.

What is a Cross Tabulation?

Cross Tabulations, or "Cross Tabs" as they are sometimes called, are a really effective analysis technique which can save time exploring data tables and help identify useful patterns in the data. A cross tabulation is a data table which displays the distribution of data of two or more variables (or questions). In simple terms, the cross tab allows the user to compare survey data responses, analysed by different questions.

Lets look at an example.

Survey

barriers q8 Report - Jan 23,2014

In this example we are looking at the results of a question (Q8) shown in the rows, against another question (Q3) which is displayed in the columns.

We can see four columns under Q3. In each table cell underneath of the columns we have the absolute number of survey participants, and two % scores. To compare the responses for Q3, we need to read down the columns. So, for the question attribute "Knowing how to phrase a question objectively", in the first column 27.3% (or 6 out of 22 cases) Strongly Agreed with the statement. If you move two columns to the right to the column "No", and look at the same rating level of Strongly Agree, we see a percentage of 21.8% or 12 out of 55 cases. We can now compare the responses of the people who say their organisation has used a survey tool with those who have not.

That's the basics for reading a cross tabulation. Running tables is a relatively easy task; the real difficulty lies in making sense of the data: analysing the data. That takes patience, experience and a degree of concentration. In this sense generating data tables should be regarded as the first step, followed by reading and digesting the data.

Raw Data

Raw Data is essentially a data file which provides a string of data which has only been partially processed for use. It is essentially a list of all the questions, and the answers provided by every survey participant (or case data) which has been collected in the survey. There are times when reading a raw data file is necessary. For example, looking at the verbatim answers given to open ended questions. We also need to look at the raw data file to review information such as the length of time it took for a survey to be completed by individual cases, as part of a quality audit. More of that in chapter 15.

But as a document to provide an analysis of survey results, the Raw Data File (or Survey Responses File), as it is called in Surveygoo, is only a partially useful file. Because the file does not analyse the data in easily read summaries of all the cases (as a Data Tabulation does, for example), it has limited use as a analytical tool.

One of the main uses of a Raw Data file, is as a file to share information with other software tools. Typically, a file exported as a CSV file, can be imported and read into other survey analysis packages. In many cases the imported file would need to be adapted and reformatted in the analysis tool, which can take time. In other cases Survey tools can export the data already formatted for a specific third party analysis tool. For example, Surveygoo has an application to export the survey data as a SPSS file, generating both the question variables and case data. There are many third party software tools available which can be sued to run more complex analysis, and validate the statistics. SPSS is one of the better known and longer established tools.

Suggested Follow Up Exercises

Look at How to Guide, Using Standard Data Tables.

Look at How to Guide, Using Custom Data Tables.

Look at How to Guide, Export Survey Responses Data.

Look at How to Guide, Using Cross Tabulations.

Data Quality

"Quality is never an accident. It is always the result of intelligent effort"

John Ruskin

The quality of survey data is absolutely of paramount importance. But what drives quality? Well, in one word, everything. Every step of the process of designing a questionnaire, and programming a survey will impact the quality of outcome. Even before the questionnaire is programmed, the design of the sample, and the approach to reaching the right audience are all vital.

One area of data quality deserves attention in its own right, and is the focus of this final chapter. The quality of panel samples.

So much of the online survey world is linked to the use of online survey panels. We can make every attempt to design and execute a carefully managed, quality survey. But if the sample used results in poor quality responses, it would have been to no avail.

Panel Quality Measures

Panel companies do their best to ensure that panels have the best quality survey participants they can.

Quality measures for many panel companies include:

▶ Quarantine rules so that survey participants do not complete too many surveys in a given period

▶ Surveys are checked to avoid language and logic issues

▶ De-duplication controls to ensure surveys are not completed twice

▶ Active quality measures to identify and remove poor quality respondents

▶ Random and stratified sampling to survey all people and not just high responders

▶ Identification measures to validate respondents

i Quarantine Rules

Some panel companies will set time restrictions so that an individual panel member cannot complete more than one survey within a defined period. The idea is to reduce potential bias of so called professional respondents, as well as reducing burn out, whereby the panel member receives too many survey invitations.

A Few Bad Eggs

And yet, there are times when some individual survey participants have not completed a survey as well as they might have. Different researchers and online research companies have different approaches towards panel quality checks. The approach may vary by survey, and there is no one size fits all approach that is optimal or better than any other.

Three Quick Market Research Panel Data Quality Checks

The following is an example of a quality test the team at Surveygoo can apply to panel surveys on behalf of clients. There are variations to the tests, but this highlights one approach. It is based on a Three Stage Quality Filter:

▶ Country Location

▶ Speed test

▶ Trap Question

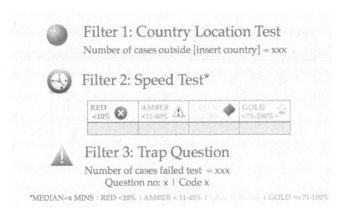

Filter 1: Country Location Test
Number of cases outside [insert country] = xxx

Filter 2: Speed Test*

RED <10%	AMBER <11-40%	GREEN	GOLD <71-100%+

Filter 3: Trap Question
Number of cases failed test = xxx
Question no: x | Code x

*MEDIAN=x MINS : RED <10% | AMBER < 11-40% | GREEN 41-40% | GOLD =<71-100%

Quality Filter 1: Country Location Test

Although panel companies take measures to limit the number of people who join a panel outside of the country where the panel is based, a minority of panel members may be resident outside the country. There is a judgement call to be made about whether some panellists have completed a survey while on holiday (this could be the case during holiday periods). But if there are too many respondents completing a survey outside the country there is a real danger of poor quality responses.

Fortunately we can identify the location of panel respondents.

In the Surveygoo survey tool, we can run an export of Survey Responses Data as a CSV file.

The Survey Responses Data File includes for each respondent (S.No). the Country, City and Region, which is taken automatically from the survey respondent's IP address.

Any cases appearing outside the intended target country can be flagged in the Survey Responses Data file, and the case data can be removed from the data set. See How to Article, Removing Case Data.

Typically, failure to meet the minimum requirements of the first quality filter, the Country Location test, means that you would remove the respondent(s) from the data set.

Quality Filter 2: Speed Test

The second stage test is the Speed Test. It is common for online survey companies to look out for so called Speeders – respondents who complete a survey too fast.

The Survey Responses Data File includes for each respondent (S.No). the Start Time and Finish Time of the survey. It also automatically calculates the Survey Duration.

There is no standard way to differentiate a speeder from a non speeder. At the margins, it must be recognised that respondents have different response times to surveys – some are able to fill out a survey more quickly than others without compromising on the quality.

So how do we differentiate speeders? Here is an approach we take at Surveygoo. First remove outliers. For example if the survey duration was estimated at 5 minutes but a respondent registered 2 hours, it should be removed from the calculation. Next, calculate the Median time of the survey duration. Excel can do this quickly using the appropriate formula. Then assign cases by comparing their duration against the Median score. We can then flag cases as follows:

- ☑ Red (10% or less than the Median)

- ☑ Amber (11-40% of the Median)

- ☑ Green (<41-70% of the Median)

- ☑ Gold (<71-100%+ of the Median)

Red cases should be flagged to be removed immediately. Gold cases are closest to the Median and should pass immediately; it is also likely that most Green cases should pass. It may also be that Amber cases will have a mix of cases we wish to keep and some to remove. But as mentioned earlier, we should not make premature judgements that the respondents who are relatively faster should be automatically regarded as poor quality respondents.

We can calibrate with one final quality check.

Quality Filter 3: Trap Question

One flexible quality check is the Trap question. Unlike the two previous tests, where the measure can be taken from data points automatically collected in the survey data, a Trap question is a manual intervention. It needs to be asked as a component of the questionnaire. It is also a non standard question. While there are many different ways we can ask a trap question, the type we recommend that makes less of an impact on programming and survey duration is to simply include an additional code in a Matrix or Drag and Drop Question. For example, a code along the lines of "Please Select Option Don't Know". If you don't have a matrix question you could include an open end question and provide an instruction, such as "Please Type the word 'Attention' in Box 3". Alternatively, if you have asked a legitimate open ended question, you can flag up respondents who have written rubbish (e.g. dhadhoahdoahdo instead of a proper answer).

Again, it doesn't mean that someone who has speeded through some questions, failed a Trap question and entered rubbish in a single open ended question should be automatically removed. But, a combination of failed tests for speeding, trap questions and rubbish data for open ended questions, make the case for removing these respondents from the data set.

Compute a Red Flag Score for all the quality checks undertaken against each of the respondents. It is recommended that the cases to be removed from the data set are agreed with Surveygoo or the panel company before proceeding to delete them.

One final thought. Online panels are not perfect but most market research panel providers genuinely want to offer the best quality panel sample they can. After all, their reputation is based on delivering quality. But we should all be aware of what panels can achieve, and their limitations. Some panel companies take more efforts than others to mitigate against poor quality panellists. Finally, online survey companies like Surveygoo can take reasonable steps to look out for suspect data. The key to success is working collaboratively with clients and panel companies to get the best result in the time and budget available.

Suggested Follow Up Exercises

Look at How to Guide, Removing Case Data.

Common Words and Phrases Used in Research

Attitudinal questions

Attitudinal questions are typically asked as rating scales, to measure brands, products, social attitudes or lifestyles. (e.g. brand attitudes such as modern, innovative, effective, value for money).

Attribute

Name commonly used to refer to an item, description or brand value in questions, e.g. brand attributes in a matrix question.

Advertising awareness

When evaluating advertising campaigns it is common to measure awareness of a brand or a specific advertising campaign, e.g. which brand of smartphones have you seen advertised recently.

Attribute association

See brand attribute.

Behavioural questions

Behavioural questions ask about what people do. They are based on fact and are usually easy to answer. It is often a good idea to place easier behavioural questions towards the beginning of a questionnaire.

Brand awareness

Spontaneous brand awareness ask for respondents recall of brands without being prompted. It is sometimes called top of mind awareness. It can be asked over several questions (e.g. which brand come to mind? Which other brands do you know. Prompted awareness offers a list of brands (e.g. Which of these brands do you know?)

Balanced scales

Any scale which has an even balance of negative and positive attitudes, e.g. very good, good, average, poor, very poor.

Brand attribute

A typical approach to measure how a brand is perceived is to show a matrix question with a list of attributes. The respondent is asked to indicate how much they agree with the brand attribute.

C

Closed question

Elicit a response to close down answers, such as "yes" and "no".

Constant Sum Scale

A question type which requires the respondent to allocate a fixed number of points between a given number of attributes, e.g. there could be five attributes and 100 points to allocate. Surveygoo shows the respondent how many points they have so they can easily reallocate points to the given total.

Customer satisfaction research

Surveys designed to measure customers perceptions of services or products.

D

Dichotomous questions

These are questions which only have two answers, e.g. Have you been to the cinema in the last month? Yes / No.

Don't Know questions

People are sometimes unsure as to whether they include a don't know response. The simple answer is that if don't know is a valid response, it should be included.

Drag and drop

Refers to question types which allow the respondent to answer the question by dragging the mouse on a grid to register their response. Are used to help improve respondent interest in the survey to vary questionnaires.

E

Exclusion questions

Sometimes organisations exclude people who work in marketing, research, advertising, etc. in case these respondents bias the results. It is no longer universal practice and not necessarily a good idea.

F

Fatigue effect

Very long or poorly presented questions can have a detrimental effect on respondent engagement and ultimately the quality of responses given. It is not recommended, for example, to have too many items in a battery of statements on a matrix question. Mixing up question styles and using drag and drop questions help respondent interest in the survey.

G

Grid questions

See Matrix questions.

H

Hypothesis development

A hypothesis is a possible answer to the research question. A hypothesis to a problem can also generate ideas to be tested in a survey.

I

Interval scales

Refers to rating scales that have an equal distance between them, e.g rating based on a numerical 10 point scale, where 1 is poor and 10 is excellent.

Itemized rating scales

Are the features, measures or attitudes which are measured on a rating scale.

J

Joint income

The income in a household, typically of a married couple or adults in a relationship. Household income levels can be targeted in Surveygoo Online Panel Access.

K

K means

A statistical technique used in cluster/segmentation analysis.

L

Likert scale

Often referred to as agree-disagree scale. Respondents see a list of attributes in a battery of statements. For each statement, the respondent indicates how much they agree with it (e.g. agree, strongly agree, disagree, strongly disagree). In Surveygoo likert scales can be set in matrix style questions. (also see Randomize).

Likelihood of purchase

A question which asks how likely a respondent would purchase a product or service on a given scale, e.g. definitely, very likely, not very likely, not at all likely.

Large scale pilot

Any large scale survey may benefit from running a trial survey to test the questionnaire and likely responses before rolling out the full surveys.

M

Multiple Choice/responses

Closed questions which have options for more than one choice are called multiple choice.

Matrix questions

Feature a grid/battery of statements or items which can rated against a scale.

N

Nominal Data

Data classified by categories or name. e.g. male, female, London, Birmingham.

Number of points on the scale

Five point scales are the most common because it is effective. It has enough points on the scale to allow discrimination and is familiar to many respondents. Seven points can be used for more discrimination (e.g. extremely likely, very likely, quite likely, neither likely nor unlikely, quite unlikely, very unlikely, extremely unlikely). 10 point scales are also common, particularly for number scales.

Numerical scale

The scale is set often between 1 and 10, or 0 and 100. The end points of the scale should be set verbally e.g. 10 at one end and 1 at the other.

Open questions

An open question does not suggest answers in the question. It could feature a short answer such as one or two products, or a longer description, such as to explain why they prefer a certain brand.

Ordinal data

Is typically found in ranking scales, where a respondent ranks the importance or attractiveness of a feature with a ranked number.

Order bias

The order in which prompts appear can have a biasing effect. Surveygoo allows you to randomize the order in which attributes appear in a grid.

Prompted questions

Questions which provide a prompt list for the respondent to review and pick an answer (e.g. Which of the following do you agree with, please rate brand x on the following scale).

Positively weighted scale

A scale which has more positive than negative dimensions, e.g. excellent, very good, good, average, poor. There is an argument for trying to differentiate higher levels of excellence in measuring customer satisfaction surveys.

Q

Questionnaire sections

When planning a questionnaire it is good practice to band subject areas together and sequence the questions in order.

Question order

It is always recommended to ask spontaneous questions before prompted questions. It is also often recommended to ask easier, general questions before asking more difficult questions.

Question flow/planning

Good questionnaire design should include planning activities to ensure that the order of questions and subject matter is mapped out before starting the scripting of surveys. Short or simple surveys can be directly designed in Surveygoo, but it is always recommended that longer questionnaires are planned in advance.

R

Rating Scale

Scales used to rate ideas or brand attributes, e.g. verbal scales such as excellent, very good, fair, etc.

Ratio scales

e.g. What proportion of your income do you spend on food? 0-5%, 6-10%, 11-15%, 16-20%, etc.

Ranking questions

Questions used to rank the order of an issue or criteria, e.g. Please rank the order of the following service criteria. Surveygoo allows you to use matrix questions or drag and drop questions where the respondent is asked to drag the factor in order of importance or attractiveness.

Routing

The means to ensure that questions are asked based on relevant answers or demographics recorded in the questionnaire, e.g. If answer yes at q3 ask q6. Surveygoo allows full routing instructions.

Randomise

It is often recommended to randomize the order of attributes in matrix questions (Likert scales). Survegoo allows you to do this. By ticking randomize in the question set up, the order of the attributes appearing to the respondents will be random, thus removing any potential bias in the order of question attributes.

S

Screening questions

If you only want to interview people with certain demographics Surrveygoo can help target relevant respondents. But sometimes it is necessary to interview people based on their behaviour or attitudes to a product or lifestyle. To do this it may be necessary to ask questions to screen out respondents, e.g. Which of the following items have you bought in the last six months? TV, DVD, iPad, Video streamer.

Spontaneous questions

Questions designed to capture a spontaneous answer (e.g. which is your preferred brand?) captures the answer in an open ended box. It is important to ensure spontaneous questions appear on pages before prompted questions appear, which could influence the answer of the spontaneous question. Typical uses of spontaneous questions include brand awareness, attitudes towards a product or advert, and likes/dislikes towards a product.

Sensitive questions

Questions which ask personal data (e.g. health, lifestyle, etc) which may be of a sensitive nature.

T

Tracking Studies

Studies which are repeated over a given period of time (e.g. monthly, quarterly, annually). Tracking studies are typically used to measure brand awareness or customer satisfaction.

U

User ability research

User tests of products in product research or to test usage of websites.

Universe

A term researchers sometimes use to refer to the size or number of organisations/respondents in a population, e.g. 500 customers in a customer database represents the universe of all the customers of an organization.

V

Verbal scales

A question scale which defines the scale with labels, e.g. Excellent, good, fair, poor instead of 4,3,2,1. Arguably, verbal scales are better for making clear what exactly the scale means.

Values

Questions which require an answer as a value or number.

W

Weighted data

Sometimes researchers weight data to match the profile of a population or customer universe.

X

Generation X

Gen X people were born after the second world war (between 1960 and early 1980s). Researchers sometimes target this audience, typically by the year they were born.

Y

Generation Y

Also known as the millennial generation, or the Millennials. Other names for Generation Y include Generation Next or Net or Echo Boomers. People born between 1980 and 1999 are often characterized as Generation Y.

Z

Generation Z

Also known as Generation M (for multi tasking) or Generation C (for connected) or Digital Natives. They are often defined as people born from 2000 onwards.